364 DAYS OF TEDIUM

364 DAYS OF TEDIUM

OR WHAT SANTA GETS UP TO ON HIS DAYS OFF

DAVE CORNMELL

THE FRIDAY PROJECT
AN IMPRINT OF HARPERCOLLINSPUBLISHERS
77-85 FULHAM PALACE ROAD
HAMMERSMITH, LONDON W6 8JB
WWW.HARPERCOLLINS.CO.UK

LOVE THIS BOOK? WWW.BOOKARMY.COM

FIRST PUBLISHED IN GREAT BRITAIN BY THE FRIDAY PROJECT IN 2010
COPYRIGHT © DAVE CORNMELL 2010

1

DAVE CORNMELL ASSERTS THE MORAL RIGHT TO
BE IDENTIFIED AS THE AUTHOR OF THIS WORK

A CATALOGUE RECORD FOR THIS BOOK
IS AVAILABLE FROM THE BRITISH LIBRARY

978-0-00-744069-6

PRINTED AND BOUND IN CHINA BY
SOUTH CHINA PRINTING COMPANY

FIND OUT MORE ABOUT HARPERCOLLINS AND THE ENVIRONMENT AT
WWW.HARPERCOLLINS.CO.UK/GREEN

CHECK OUT SANTA ON:

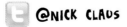 @NICK CLAUS   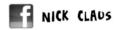 DAYSOFTEDIUM   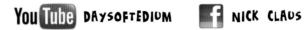 NICK CLAUS

FOR JACKIE, ELEANOR AND EMILY

25TH DECEMBER

364 DAYS OFF WORK! I CAN DO ANYTHING I WANT!

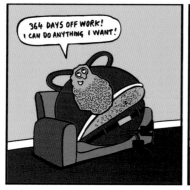

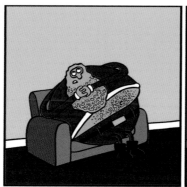

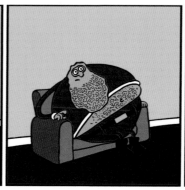

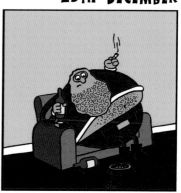

26TH DECEMBER

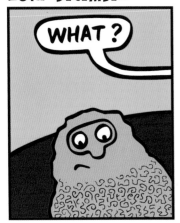

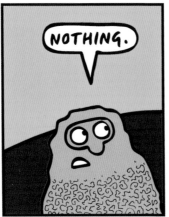

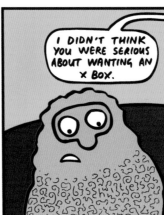

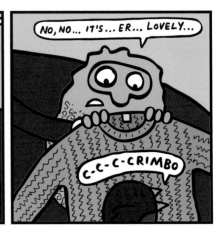

27TH DECEMBER

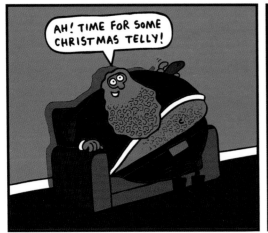

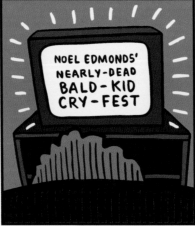

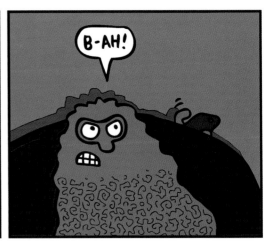

28TH DECEMBER

NICK! NICK!
AHH! WHAT IS IT?
IT'S SNOWING!
IT'S ALWAYS SNOWING!
I KNOW, I LIKE SNOW

29TH DECEMBER

IF PEOPLE STOP BELIEVING IN ME, WILL I CEASE TO EXIST?
NO... IT'S OK... I STILL BELIEVE IN ME!
DON'T I?

30TH DECEMBER

DUCKY & MR. WHALE

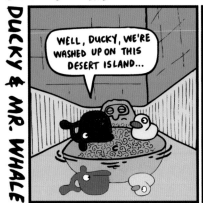

WELL, DUCKY, WE'RE WASHED UP ON THIS DESERT ISLAND...

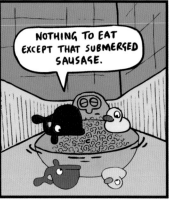

NOTHING TO EAT EXCEPT THAT SUBMERGED SAUSAGE.

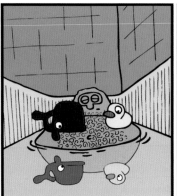

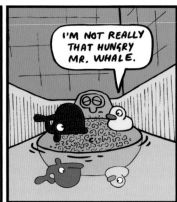

I'M NOT REALLY THAT HUNGRY MR. WHALE.

31ST DECEMBER

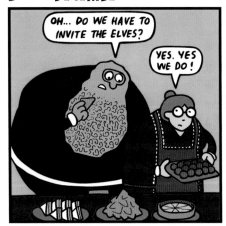

OH... DO WE HAVE TO INVITE THE ELVES?

YES. YES WE DO!

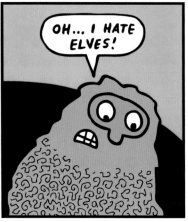

OH... I HATE ELVES!

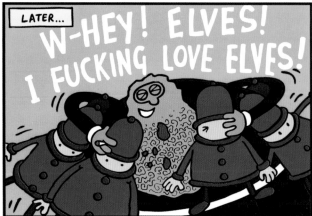

LATER...

W-HEY! ELVES! I FUCKING LOVE ELVES!

1ST JANUARY

2ND JANUARY

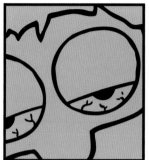

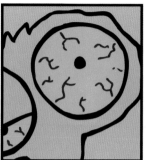

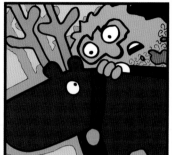

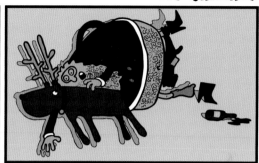

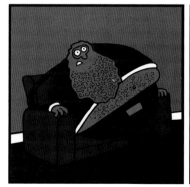

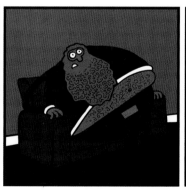

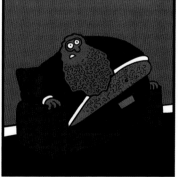

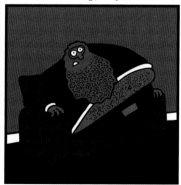

3RD JANUARY

OH... ER... I HAD TO LET VIXEN GO...
YEAH... ER... SHE WAS ERM... STEALING...
UM... ER... STATIONARY?
AH WELL, NEVER MIND.
YEAH... YEAH... I WAS GUTTED TOO... OBVIOUSLY.

4TH JANUARY

GYM
WOW! I FORGOT WE HAD A GYM!
AND A CAT.
CLICK!

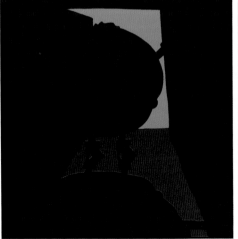

5TH JANUARY

RIGHT, TIME TO TAKE THESE DECORATIONS DOWN!
SOD THIS!

6TH JANUARY

MARY! THE LIGHT IN THE SHITTER'S BROKEN!
MARY! MARY!!
YOU MIGHT WANT TO BRING UP SOME MORE AIR FRESHENER TOO!

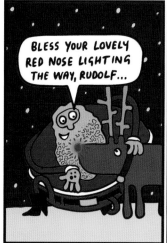

BLESS YOUR LOVELY RED NOSE LIGHTING THE WAY, RUDOLF...

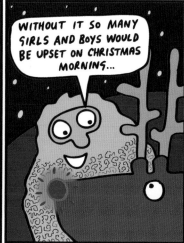

WITHOUT IT SO MANY GIRLS AND BOYS WOULD BE UPSET ON CHRISTMAS MORNING...

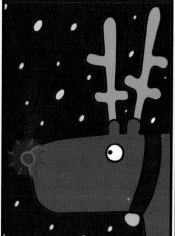

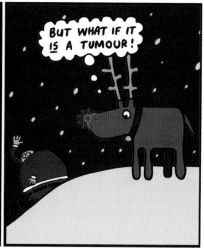

BUT WHAT IF IT IS A TUMOUR!

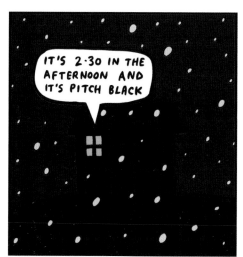

IT'S 2·30 IN THE AFTERNOON AND IT'S PITCH BLACK

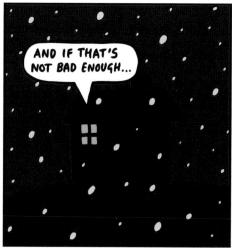

AND IF THAT'S NOT BAD ENOUGH...

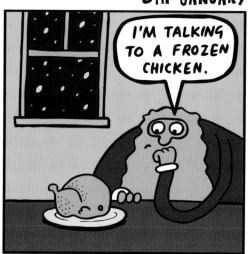

I'M TALKING TO A FROZEN CHICKEN.

9TH JANUARY

I COULD GET UP AND SORT THAT LEAKY TAP OUT...
I COULD GET UP AND CLEAR THE DRIVE...
OR I COULD...
ZZZZZZZ

10TH JANUARY

YOU'RE FLOATING!
YES, I KNOW THAT...
ANY IDEA HOW I GET DOWN?

P-LPP!
PL-PPP!
P-LPP!
PL-PPP!
I THINK I NEED A HOLIDAY.

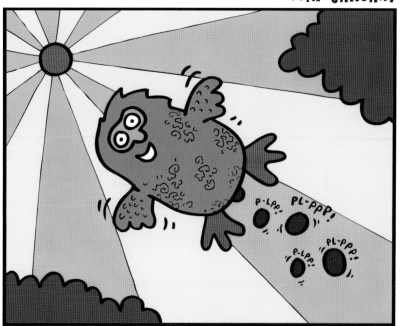

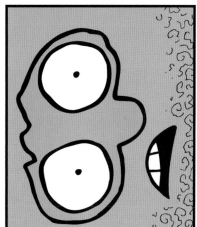

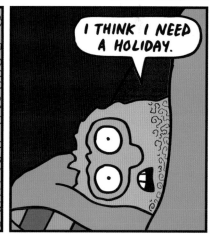

12TH JANUARY

AGHH! I REALLY NEED THE LOO BUT IT'S A BLIZZARD OUT THERE!
OOOOOHH!
AAAAGHHH!!

13TH JANUARY

THE FITNESS REGIME STARTS TODAY...
SQUAT!!
RIP!!
FART!
RIGHT AFTER I CHANGE MY TROUSERS...

14TH JANUARY

N-URGHH!!
AAGHHH!!
HOW MANY'S THAT?
NONE.

15TH JANUARY

BLURSH!!!
HOW'S THE EXERCISE BIKE?
YEAH, GOOD - I JUST LOST THREE POUNDS!

16TH JANUARY

MMMMM!!
LOVELY, PURE ICICLE WATER!

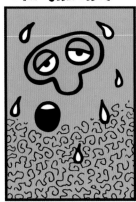

17TH JANUARY

MARY! I THINK I'VE FOUND A LUMP ON MY ARSE!
LOOK!
ER... THAT'S A HALF-EATEN KING PRAWN.
I'VE TOLD YOU ABOUT EATING TAKEAWAYS IN BED.

18TH JANUARY

FOR CRYING OUT LOUD!
OI!
STOP HAVING SEX WITH MY SATELLITE DISH!

19TH JANUARY

WE'RE GOING TO HOLD AUDITIONS TO PICK VIXEN'S REPLACEMENT...
EVERYONE HAS A CHANCE TO MAKE NEXT YEAR'S SLEIGH TEAM...
EXCEPT TERRY OBVIOUSLY...
IT'S NOT LIKE WE'RE HIGH OR SOMETHING.

20TH JANUARY

21ST JANUARY

DUCKY & MR. WHALE

HAVE YOU EVER WONDERED WHAT OUR OFFSPRING WOULD BE LIKE IF WE MATED?
YUK!
KILL IT!
BEST NOT TO FIND OUT, EH?

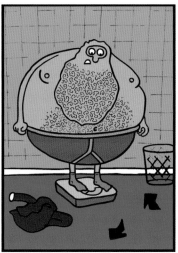

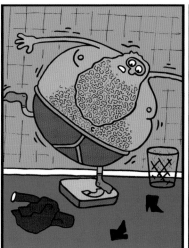

22ND JANUARY

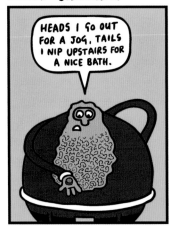

HEADS I GO OUT FOR A JOG, TAILS I NIP UPSTAIRS FOR A NICE BATH.

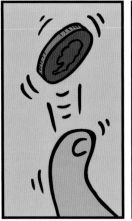

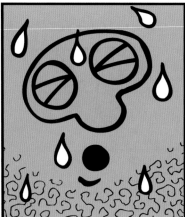

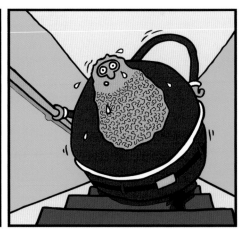

23RD JANUARY

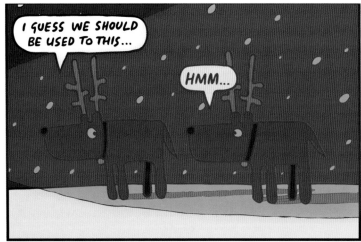

I GUESS WE SHOULD BE USED TO THIS...

HMM...

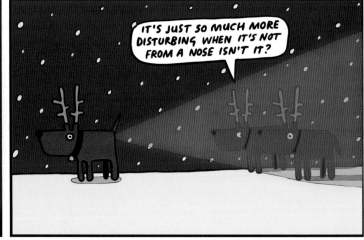

IT'S JUST SO MUCH MORE DISTURBING WHEN IT'S NOT FROM A NOSE ISN'T IT?

24TH JANUARY

YOGA
HOW HARD CAN IT BE?
OH HELLO...
IS THAT THE CHIROPRACTOR?

25TH JANUARY

CRACK!
IS THAT THE FITNESS REGIME DONE THEN?
YES!

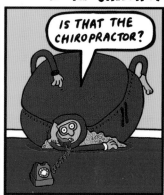

26TH JANUARY

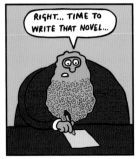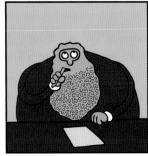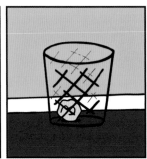

27TH JANUARY

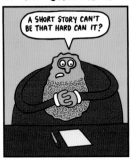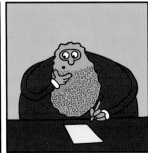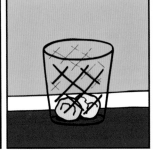

28TH JANUARY

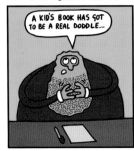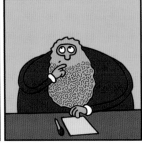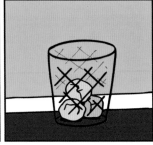

29TH JANUARY

MAYBE I COULD TRY POETRY...

30TH JANUARY

THAT'S IT!
ALL DONE!
EGGS
BREAD
MILK
CHEESE
LOTTO

31ST JANUARY

HAVE YOU MUCKED OUT THE REINDEER RECENTLY?
ER... YES... OF COURSE...

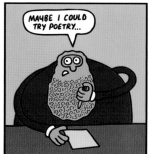

1ST FEBRUARY

THAT'S IT! NO MORE BOOZE FOR A MONTH!
YAY!

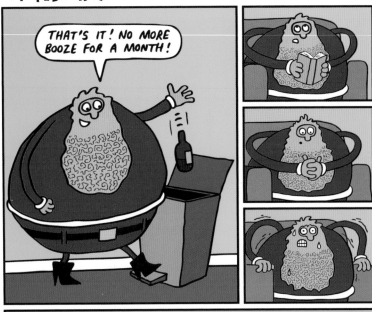

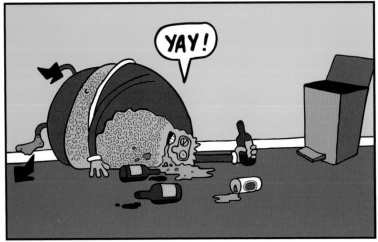

WELL, YOU CERTAINLY FIT ALL THE CRITERIA FOR TAKING OVER FROM VIXEN...
STRONG, HARD-WORKING, DILLIGENT...
JUST ONE THING REALLY...
WOULD YOU MIND CHANGING YOUR NAME FROM SHITBISCUIT?

3RD FEBRUARY

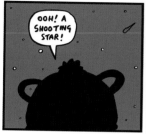 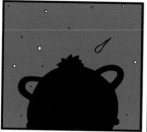 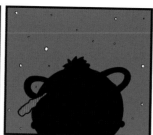 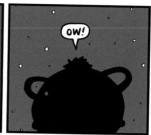

4TH FEBRUARY

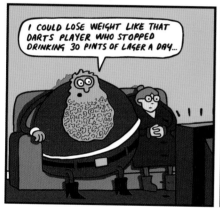 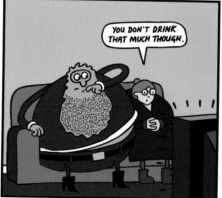 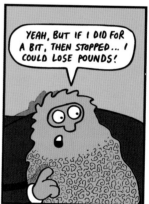

5TH FEBRUARY

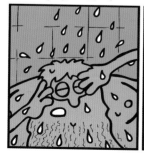 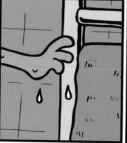 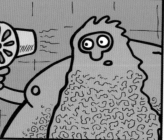 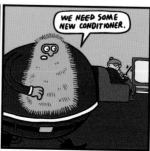

6TH FEBRUARY

AH, MR SNOWMAN! ALWAYS SO HAPPY AND CHEERFUL!
IT'S FUNNY YOU SHOULD SAY THAT. YOU SEE; MY MOUTH MIGHT BE FIXED IN A PERMANENT GRIN...
...BUT I'M ACTUALLY IN TREMENDOUS PAIN!
KILL ME!

7TH FEBRUARY

P-AHH!
IF I GET ONE MORE LETTER ASKING FOR 'MUMMY + DADDY BACK TOGETHER'...

8TH FEBRUARY

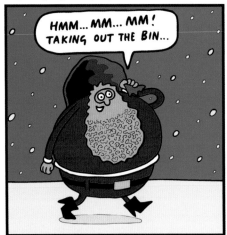

HMM... MM... MM! TAKING OUT THE BIN...

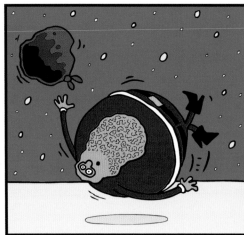

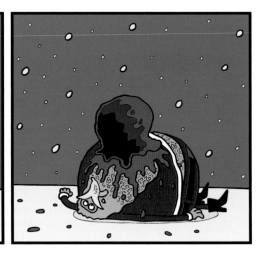

9TH FEBRUARY

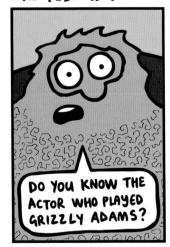

DO YOU KNOW THE ACTOR WHO PLAYED GRIZZLY ADAMS?

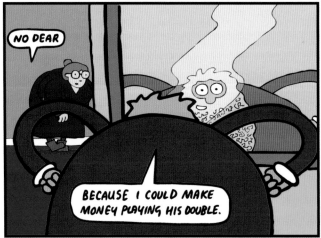

NO DEAR

BECAUSE I COULD MAKE MONEY PLAYING HIS DOUBLE.

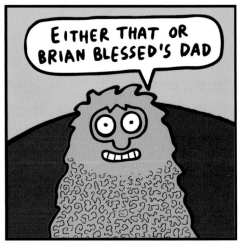

EITHER THAT OR BRIAN BLESSED'S DAD

10TH FEBRUARY

CLUNK!

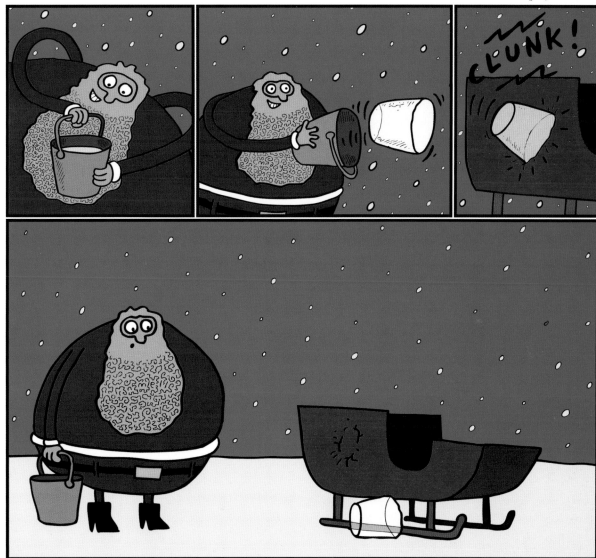

11TH FEBRUARY

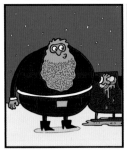 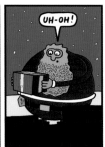 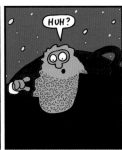

12TH FEBRUARY

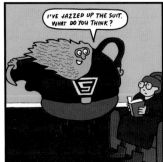 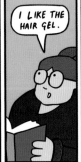 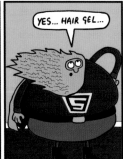 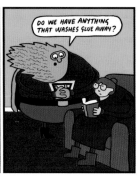

13TH FEBRUARY

14TH FEBRUARY

CAN YOU REMEMBER THE LAST TIME WE DID IT ?
I'M NOT EVEN SURE I'D KNOW WHAT TO DO ANYMORE...
I'LL MAKE US A NICE CUP OF TEA SHALL I ?

15TH FEBRUARY

HAS SANTA EVER TOUCHED YOU ?
HOW DO YOU MEAN?
YOU KNOW... SEXUALLY ?
NO! GOD NO! WHY HAS HE TOUCHED YOU?
NO... NO... OF COURSE NOT...
I WISH HE WOULD THOUGH...
I THINK HE'S HOT.

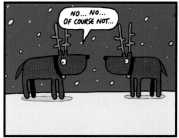

16TH FEBRUARY

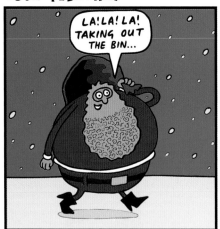
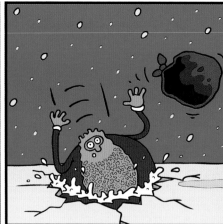
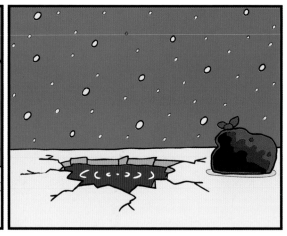

17TH FEBRUARY

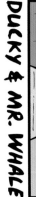

DUCKY & MR. WHALE

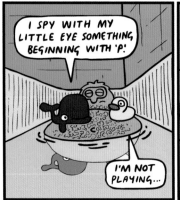
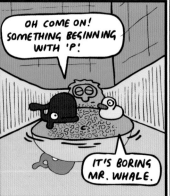
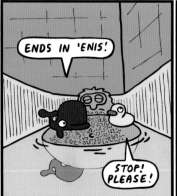
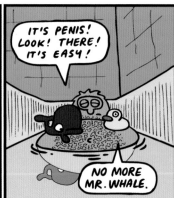

18TH FEBRUARY

HMM... WHERE TO GO ON HOLIDAY THIS YEAR?
PORTUGAL? OK... LET'S SEE...
POR
POR
N
SO IS THE HOLIDAY BOOKED THEN?
ER... UM... NO...
THE INTERNET WAS... ERM...
...CLOSED?

19TH FEBRUARY

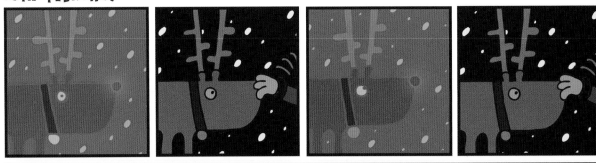

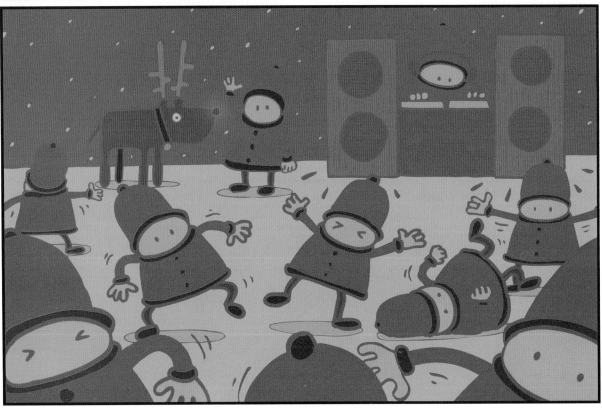

20TH FEBRUARY

UR-RGHHH!!
GGG-RRR!!!
AAGHHHHH!!
YOU HAVE TO GET A NORMAL SIZE TABLE.

21ST FEBRUARY

AH, BIN DAY!
RIP!

22ND FEBRUARY

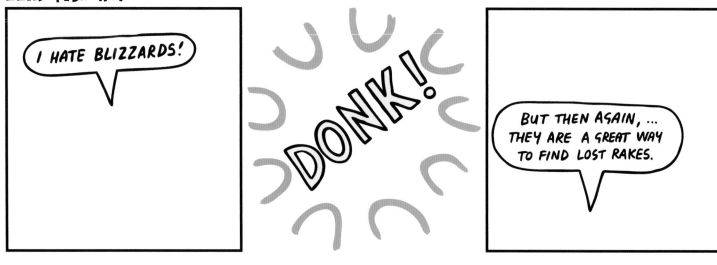

23RD FEBRUARY

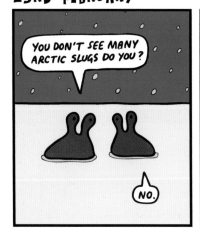 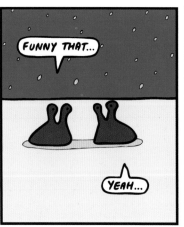 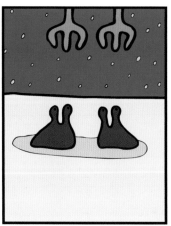 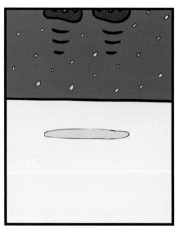

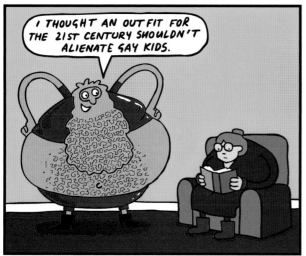

I THOUGHT AN OUTFIT FOR THE 21ST CENTURY SHOULDN'T ALIENATE GAY KIDS.

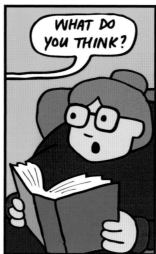

WHAT DO YOU THINK?

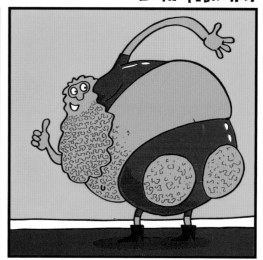

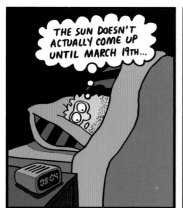

THE SUN DOESN'T ACTUALLY COME UP UNTIL MARCH 19TH...

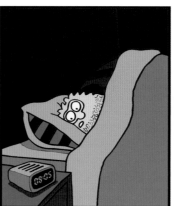

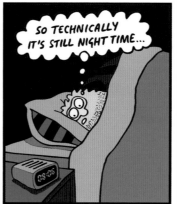

SO TECHNICALLY IT'S STILL NIGHT TIME...

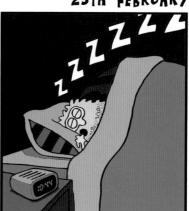

ZZZZZZ

26TH FEBRUARY

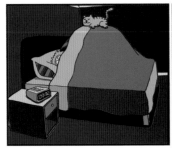 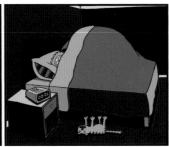 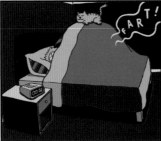

27TH FEBRUARY

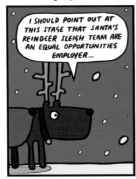 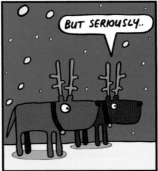 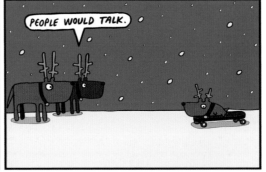

28TH FEBRUARY

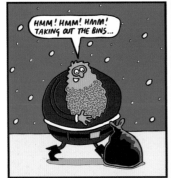 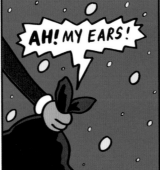 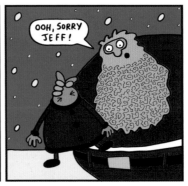

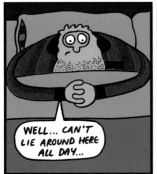

WELL... CAN'T LIE AROUND HERE ALL DAY...

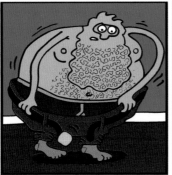

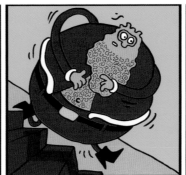

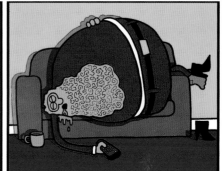

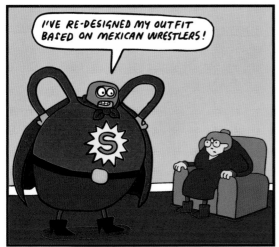

I'VE RE-DESIGNED MY OUTFIT BASED ON MEXICAN WRESTLERS!

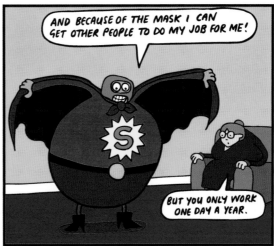

AND BECAUSE OF THE MASK I CAN GET OTHER PEOPLE TO DO MY JOB FOR ME!

BUT YOU ONLY WORK ONE DAY A YEAR.

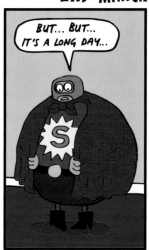

BUT... BUT... IT'S A LONG DAY...

3RD MARCH

WHAT'S MY TO-DO LIST?
FIX THAT TAP...
CLEAR THE DRIVE...
BUT FIRST THINGS FIRST...
FINALLY GET OFF THE FLOOR.

DUCKY & MR. WHALE

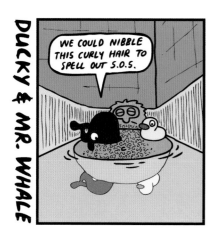

WE COULD NIBBLE THIS CURLY HAIR TO SPELL OUT S.O.S.

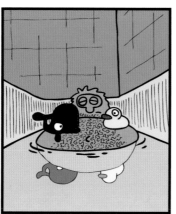

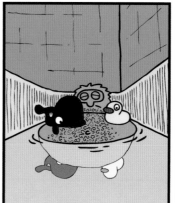

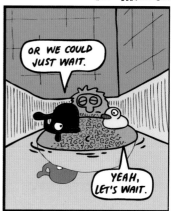

OR WE COULD JUST WAIT.

YEAH, LET'S WAIT.

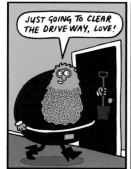

JUST GOING TO CLEAR THE DRIVEWAY, LOVE!

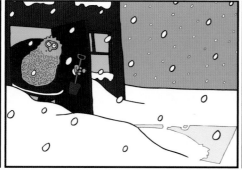

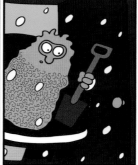

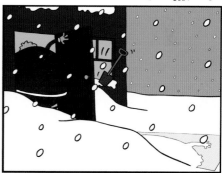

6TH MARCH

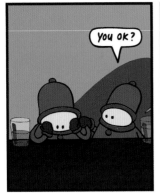

YOU OK?

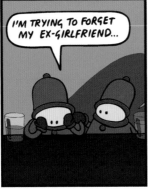

I'M TRYING TO FORGET MY EX-GIRLFRIEND...

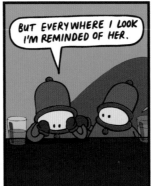

BUT EVERYWHERE I LOOK I'M REMINDED OF HER.

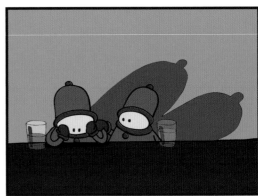

7TH MARCH

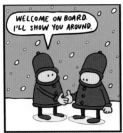

WELCOME ON BOARD. I'LL SHOW YOU AROUND.

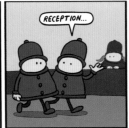

RECEPTION...

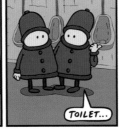

TOILET...

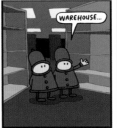

WAREHOUSE...

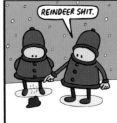

REINDEER SHIT.

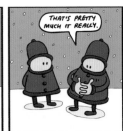

THAT'S PRETTY MUCH IT REALLY.

8TH MARCH

TERRY! TERRY! IT'S TOO FOGGY TO FLY THE SLEIGH!
THEY TOLD ME TO GET YOU...
...TO GO AND FIND RUDOLF.

9TH MARCH

IS IT ALWAYS LIKE THIS?
NO...
NO... SOMETIMES I SLEEP UNDER THE DESK.

10TH MARCH

DO I HAVE TO FILL IN A TAX FORM?
NO LOVE...
CHEESE
DO YOUR TAX NOW!
... FICTIONAL CHARACTERS DON'T PAY TAX.
CHEESE
DO YOUR TAX NOW!

11TH MARCH

YOU SHOULD TREAT YOURSELF...
YAY. I GOT A GOAL!
THE NEWS
WORLD GETTING HOTTER!
I'M FINE...
YAY. I GOT A GOAL!
THE NEWS
WORLD GETTING HOTTER!
... BUT THERE'S A SALE ON AND EVERYTHING.
YAY. I GOT A GOAL!
THE NEWS
WORLD GETTING HOTTER!
FOR THE LAST TIME, I DON'T NEED NEW GLASSES
POLAR EXPEDITION
BIG BIG THINGS

12TH MARCH

OOH! THAT'S NICE!
IT'S SUPPOSED TO BE A COFFEE TABLE...

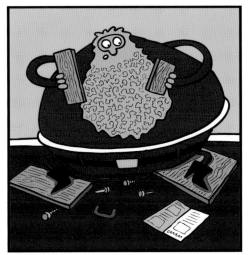

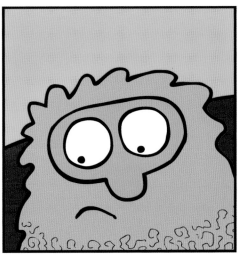

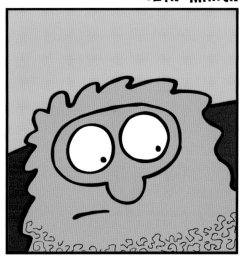

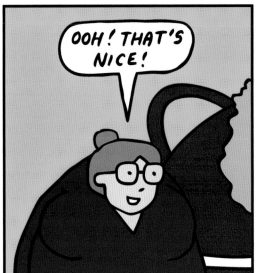

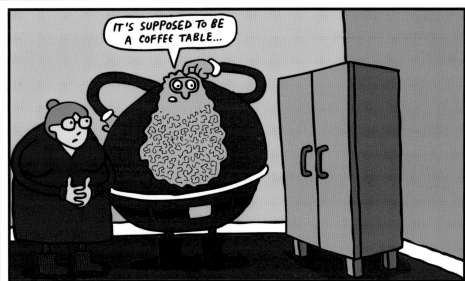

13TH MARCH

DING-DONG!
DING-DONG!
COMING!
HANG ON!
ARSES!

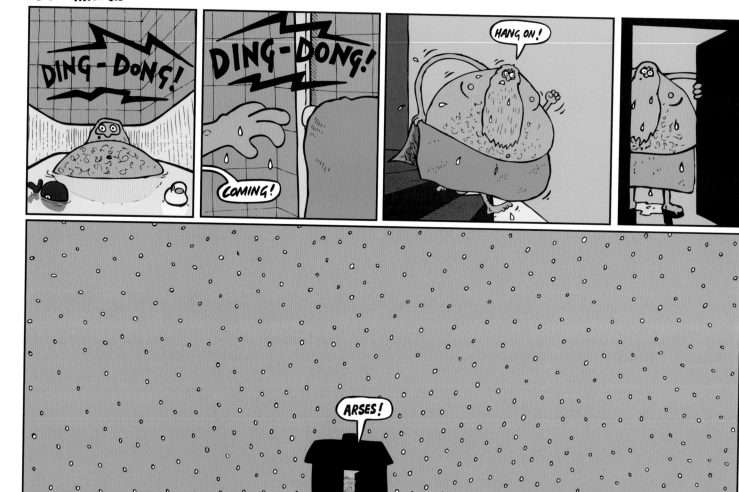

14TH MARCH

WE'RE MORE THAN IMPRESSED WITH YOUR PHYSICAL ATTRIBUTES...
WE'RE JUST NOT SURE HOW IT MAKES YOU A GOOD REPLACEMENT FOR VIXEN.

15TH MARCH

...IRAQ... ...RECESSION... AFGHANISTAN...
TV MAKES ME SO ANGRY!
CLICK!
AND YET SO HAPPY!
ONE HUNDRED AND EIGHTY!

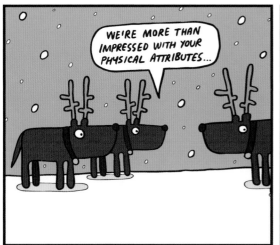

16TH MARCH

OW! MY HEAD!
WHAT WAS I DRINKING LAST NIGHT?
GIN
GLUE
YEAH, FAIR ENOUGH...

17TH MARCH

RUDOLPH!

18TH MARCH

CAN YOU STOP THAT ?
IT'S REALLY UNPLEASANT.

19TH MARCH

BRILLIANT! TODAY IS THE FIRST DAY OF SUMMER!
ALLEGEDLY.

20TH MARCH

MAYBE IT'S TIME FOR A NEW HAIRSTYLE?...

21ST MARCH

IT'S NO GOOD...
I'LL BE A LAUGHING STOCK...
I CAN'T GO OUT LIKE THIS.
YOU COULD ALWAYS WEAR A HAT.

22ND MARCH

MARY'S RIGHT... A HAT MIGHT BE THE ANSWER...
IT'LL HAVE TO DO...

23RD MARCH

DUCKY & MR. WHALE

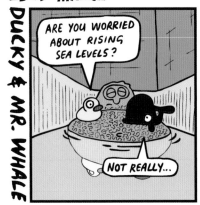
ARE YOU WORRIED ABOUT RISING SEA LEVELS?

NOT REALLY...

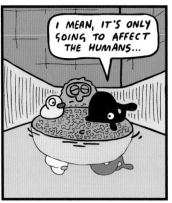
I MEAN, IT'S ONLY GOING TO AFFECT THE HUMANS...

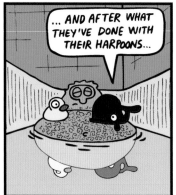
... AND AFTER WHAT THEY'VE DONE WITH THEIR HARPOONS...

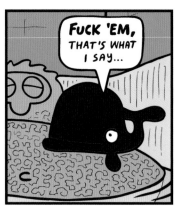
FUCK 'EM, THAT'S WHAT I SAY...

24TH MARCH

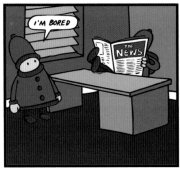
I'M BORED

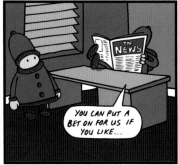
YOU CAN PUT A BET ON FOR US IF YOU LIKE...

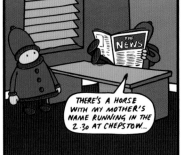
THERE'S A HORSE WITH MY MOTHER'S NAME RUNNING IN THE 2.30 AT CHEPSTOW...

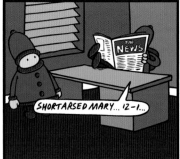
SHORTARSED MARY... 12-1...

25TH MARCH

DID I SWITCH THE GAS OFF?
YES... BUT WHAT ABOUT THE FRONT DOOR?
I THINK IT'S LOCKED, BUT THEN...
AM I WEARING PANTS?
YEP! STILL GOT IT!

26TH MARCH

COME ON!
GROW YOU BASTARD!
GROW!
SNAP!
YOU BASTARD!

27TH MARCH

THAT'S IT! GROW MY LOVELIES!

28TH MARCH

WHY ARE WE SO WHITE MUM?
IT'S SO WE CAN BLEND IN WITH OUR SURROUNDINGS AND SNEAK UPON OUR...
SHIT! WHERE ARE YOU?
PHEW! THERE YOU ARE!

29TH MARCH

GG-NN-AAGHH!!
COLD!
I'LL BE PISSING WITH TWEEZERS AGAIN TONIGHT!

30TH MARCH

CREEK!
CREEK!
URGH!
THE THOUGHT OF THOSE TWO GOING AT IT PUTS ME RIGHT OFF THIS RAT CARCASS

31ST MARCH

YOU KNOW WHAT I LOVE ABOUT BEING A MAGGOT?
WHAT?
THE HOURS.

1ST APRIL

THIS IS THE LIFE ISN'T IT?
YEAH... YEAH...
IF YOU'RE A MAGGOT, LIKE.
YEAH... THIS WOULD BE RUBBISH IF YOU WERE AN ARTS GRADUATE OR SOMETHING.

2ND APRIL

ANY PLANS FOR THE WEEKEND?
I THOUGHT I MIGHT CHEW THROUGH THE SCROTAL SACK. HOW ABOUT YOU?
OH, I MIGHT HAVE A GO AT THE EYE BALLS AND NASAL CAVITY...
GOD DAVE - YOU'RE SUCH A YUPPIE!

3RD APRIL

DAVE?
DAVE! NO!

4TH APRIL

DUCKY & MR. WHALE

AH, THERE YOU ARE!
THE HORROR... THE HORROR...

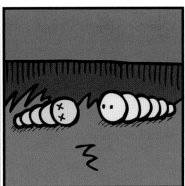

5TH APRIL

I'VE CALLED YOU TOGETHER BECAUSE THERE'S A SCIENTIFIC EXPEDITION ON THE WAY.
YOU KNOW THE DRILL...
PAINT
AND REMEMBER - NOT A WORD! THEY CAN'T KNOW WE'RE HERE.

6TH APRIL

7TH APRIL

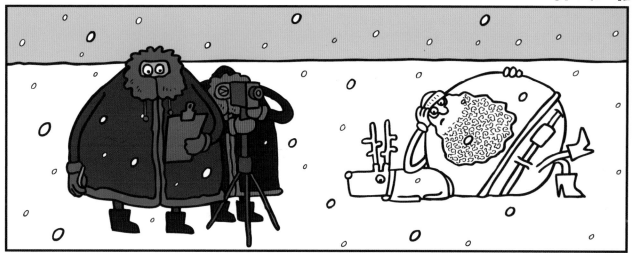

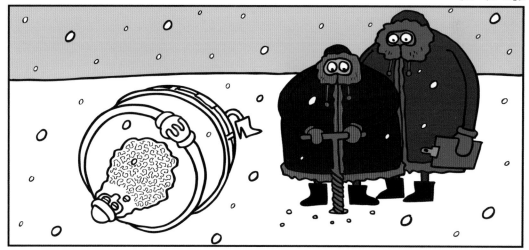

8TH APRIL

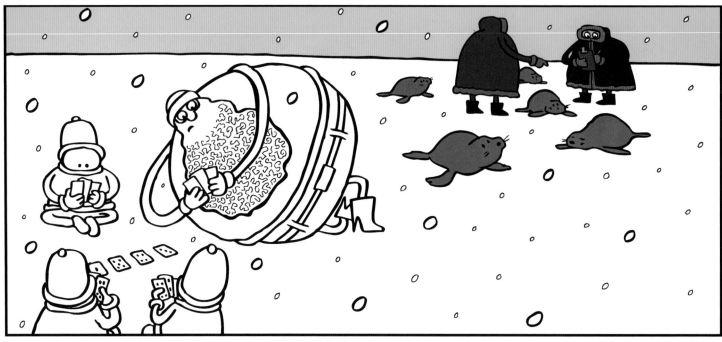

oOOP!
CAN YOU TRY AND BE A LITTLE LESS CLUMSY?

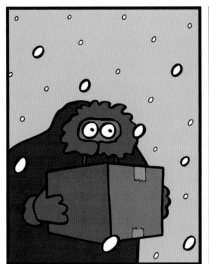

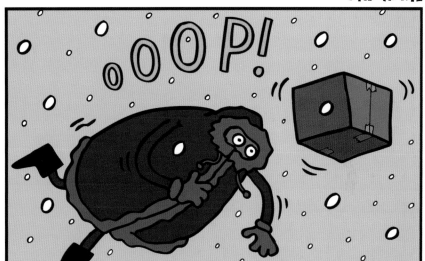

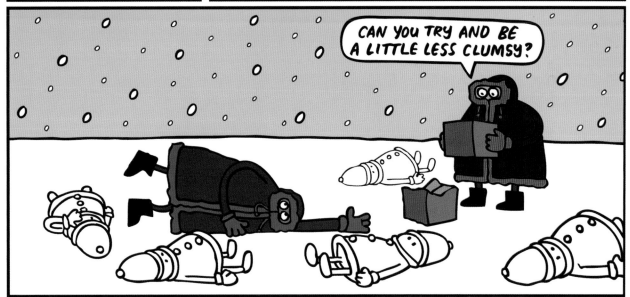

10TH APRIL

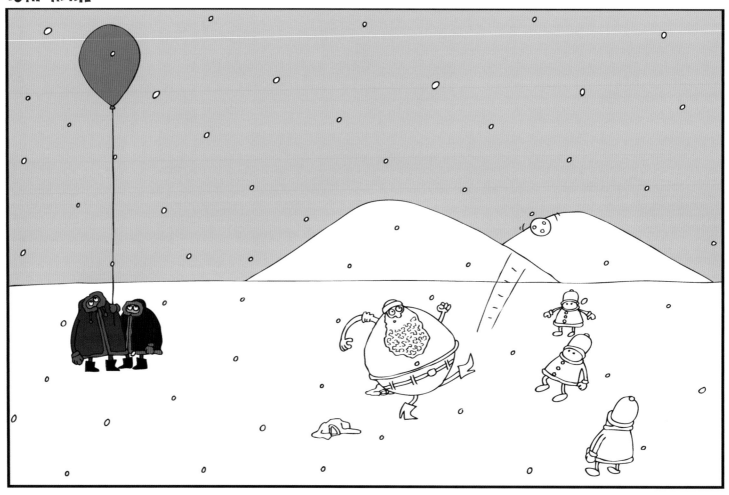

11TH APRIL

THAT'S ODD...
IT'S LIKE HE'S HAVING A FIT OR SOMETHING.

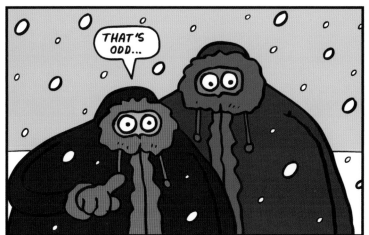

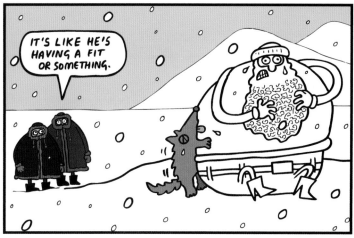

12TH APRIL

DO WE REALLY NEED THE GUN?
WHAT YOU DON'T REALISE IS THAT POLAR BEARS COULD BE STANDING RIGHT NEXT TO US AND WE WOULDN'T KNOW UNTIL IT'S TOO LATE.
SO YES... WE NEED THE GUN

13TH APRIL

WHAT'S THAT?
WHAT?
THAT THERE!
I DO BELIEVE THAT'S AN ARCTIC TERN

14TH APRIL

YOU KNOW, TO THE UNTRAINED EYE IT'S KIND OF BORING AROUND HERE.

15TH APRIL

FART!!
THEY'RE CUTE... BUT THEY DON'T HALF STINK...

16TH APRIL

IT MUST BE THE MAGNETIC FORCE OF THE POLE...
IT'S THE ONLY WAY I CAN EXPLAIN SNOW DRIFTING SO STRANGELY

17TH APRIL

WELL, THAT'S A FIRST.
YEP.
I'VE NEVER SEEN A HUSKIE PEEING AGAINST NOTHING BEFORE.

18TH APRIL

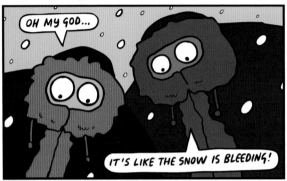

OH MY GOD...

IT'S LIKE THE SNOW IS BLEEDING!

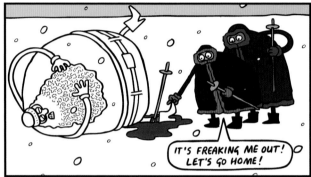

IT'S FREAKING ME OUT! LET'S GO HOME!

19TH APRIL

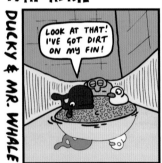

LOOK AT THAT! I'VE GOT DIRT ON MY FIN!

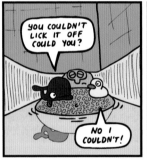

YOU COULDN'T LICK IT OFF COULD YOU?

NO I COULDN'T!

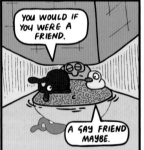

YOU WOULD IF YOU WERE A FRIEND.

A GAY FRIEND MAYBE.

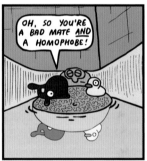

OH, SO YOU'RE A BAD MATE _AND_ A HOMOPHOBE!

20TH APRIL

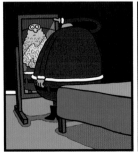

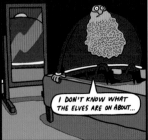

I DON'T KNOW WHAT THE ELVES ARE ON ABOUT...

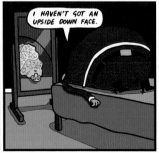

I HAVEN'T GOT AN UPSIDE DOWN FACE.

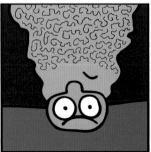

21ST APRIL

I'M A FLY!
THOSE MONTHS OF BEING A WORTHLESS MAGGOT ARE OVER!
GRAVITY CANNOT HOLD ME! I'M FREE TO GO WHEREVER I CHOOSE!
OH, THE IRONY!

22ND APRIL

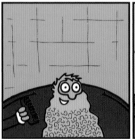 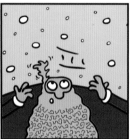 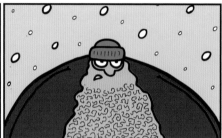

23RD APRIL

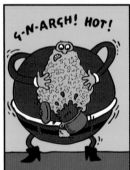 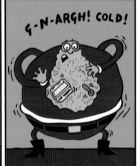 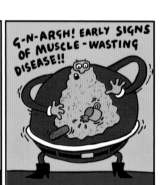

24TH APRIL

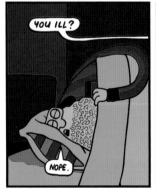 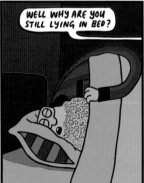 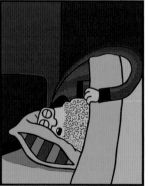 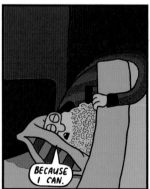

25TH APRIL

YOU CAN'T STAY IN BED FOREVER.
JUST WATCH ME.

26TH APRIL

URGH!

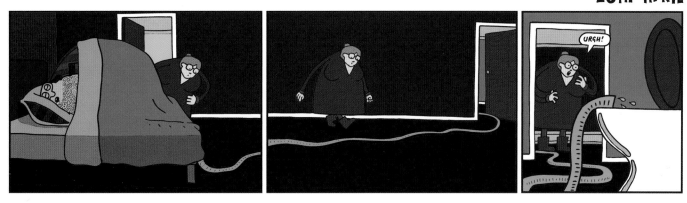

27TH APRIL

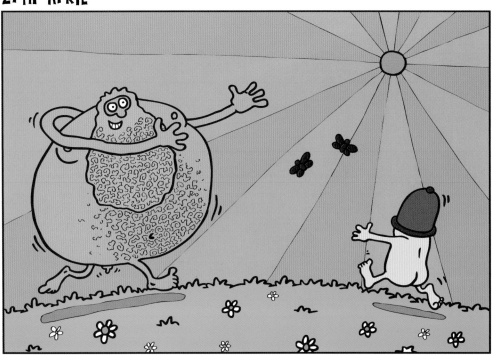

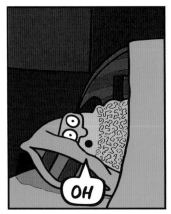

OH
MY
GOD!

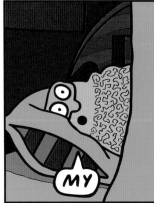

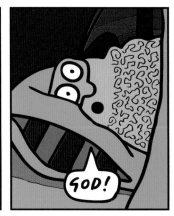

28TH APRIL

HMM... THIS IS THE BEST MASSAGE EVER!
YOU'RE VERY WELCOME, DARLING

29TH APRIL

OK... HE'S NOT UNDER THE DUVET...
...HE'S NOT UNDER THE BED...
HE'S NOT REAL!
OH YES I AM!

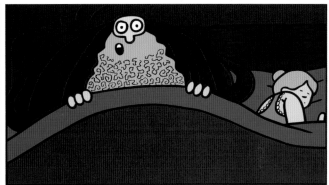

30TH APRIL

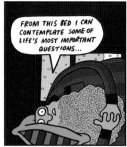

FROM THIS BED I CAN CONTEMPLATE SOME OF LIFE'S MOST IMPORTANT QUESTIONS...

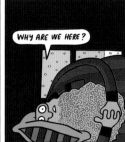

WHY ARE WE HERE?

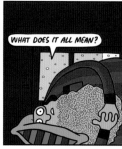

WHAT DOES IT ALL MEAN?

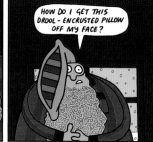

HOW DO I GET THIS DROOL-ENCRUSTED PILLOW OFF MY FACE?

1ST MAY

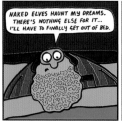

NAKED ELVES HAUNT MY DREAMS. THERE'S NOTHING ELSE FOR IT... I'LL HAVE TO FINALLY GET OUT OF BED.

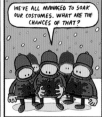

WE'VE ALL MANAGED TO SOAK OUR COSTUMES. WHAT ARE THE CHANCES OF THAT?

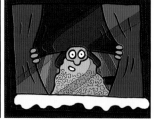

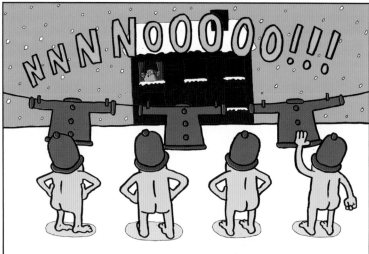

NNNNOOOOO!!!

2ND MAY

OH GOD! NOT ANOTHER WEIRD DREAM!
WAIT... NO... I'VE BEEN SLEEP WALKING AGAIN...

3RD MAY

I'LL CLOSE MY EYES AND WHEREVER I POINT IS WHERE WE'RE GOING ON HOLIDAY...
THAT WAS JUST A PRACTICE RUN, RIGHT?

4TH MAY

COME ON MARY!
WE DON'T WANT TO MISS THE FLIGHT!
I DREAD TO THINK HOW YOU'D BE IF WE EVER HAD TO GET TO AN AIRPORT.

5TH MAY

GREENLAND
LONDON
PARIS
WOULD IT KILL YOU TO WAIT UNTIL WE GET THERE BEFORE YOU START DRINKING?
BUT I'M ON MY HOLIDAYS!

6TH MAY

RIGHT, ARE WE READY FOR THE BEACH?
I'M NOT GOING ANYWHERE WITH YOU LOOKING LIKE THAT!
BUT IT'S WHAT THEY ALL WEAR OUT HERE!

7TH MAY

HEE! HEE! I'M GOING SKINNY DIPPING!
TRIP!
I THINK IT'S A WHALE

8TH MAY

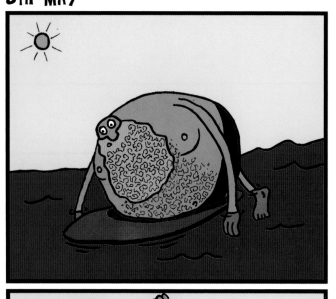

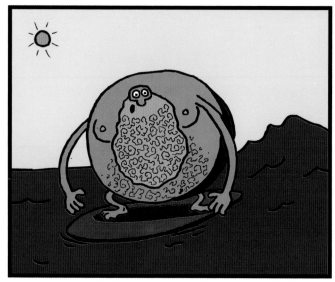

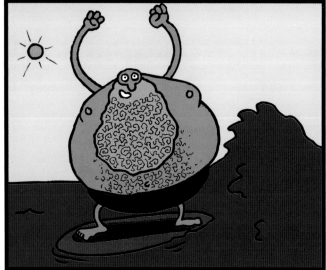

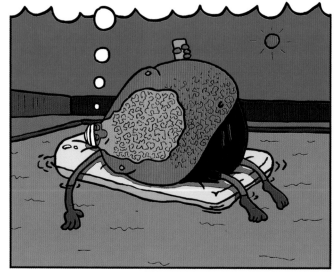

9TH MAY

IT'S NICE TO GET AWAY...
HAVE A BREAK FROM THE OLD ROUTINE.
AYE!

10TH MAY

AH!
THIS IS THE LIFE!

11TH MAY

SNIFF!!
CAN YOU SMELL ROAST PORK?
NO...

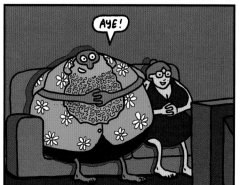

12TH MAY

RUDOLF?
SORRY LOVE - DIDN'T MEAN TO WAKE YOU... I WAS JUST POPPING TO THE LOO.

13TH MAY

AAAAARR-
RRRRRR
RRRRRRRR
SSSSSSSS
OW!

14TH MAY

HAVE YOU BEEN SNORKLING AGAIN?
HOW DID YOU GUESS?

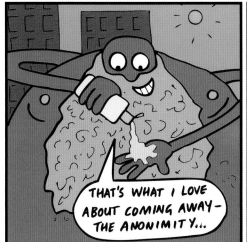

THAT'S WHAT I LOVE ABOUT COMING AWAY— THE ANONIMITY...

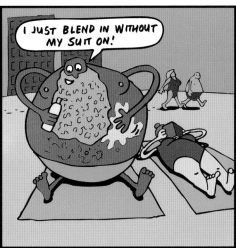

I JUST BLEND IN WITHOUT MY SUIT ON!

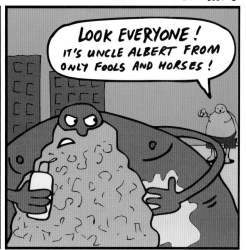

LOOK EVERYONE! IT'S UNCLE ALBERT FROM ONLY FOOLS AND HORSES!

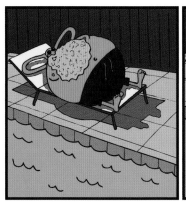

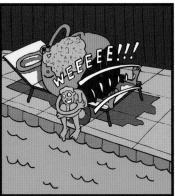

WEEEEEE!!!

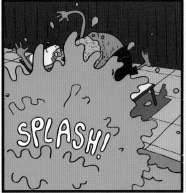

SPLASH!

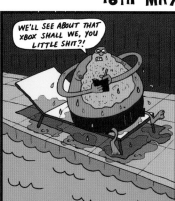

WE'LL SEE ABOUT THAT XBOX SHALL WE, YOU LITTLE SHIT?!

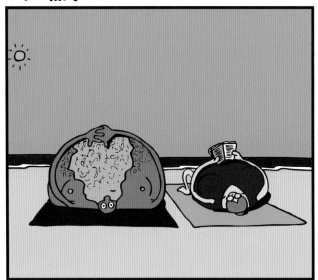

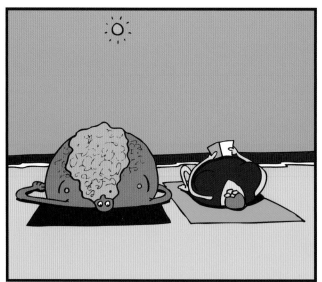

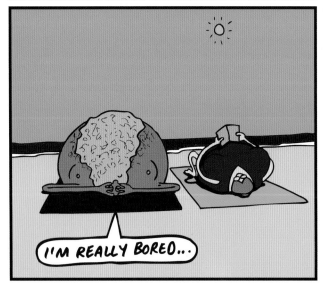

I'M REALLY BORED...

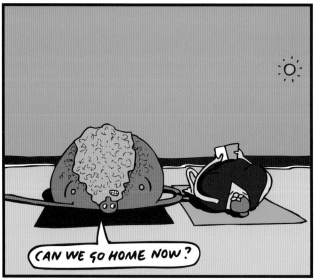

CAN WE GO HOME NOW?

18TH MAY

I'M BORED!
BORED! BORED! BORED! BORED! BORED!
IF YOU'RE LOOKING FOR SOMETHING TO DO YOU COULD ALWAYS PUT UP SOME SHELVES.
H-RUMFF!

19TH MAY

DDDDRRRRI'LLL!!
ARSES!

20TH MAY

PERFECT!

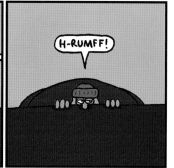

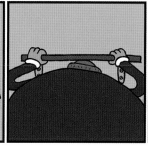

21ST MAY

HMMM...
JUST NEEDS A FEW MILLIMETRES OFF THE SIDES...
ARSES!

22ND MAY

NICK
NICK,
going away
a while.
'll have
to look after
yourself for a
bit, Mary -x-
NNNOOOOO!!

23RD MAY

PING!
0:00

24TH MAY

MMM... WHAT SHALL I HAVE FOR DINNER?
LASAGNE? NO... TOO TIME CONSUMING...
CHILLI
LASAGNE
CURRY? NO... LOOKS A BIT TOO HARD...
THERE MUST BE SOMETHING EASIER...
BREA

25TH MAY

TALK TO ME!
PLEASE! I'M BEGGING YOU!!
TELL ME WHAT I'M SUPPOSED TO DO WITH YOU!!

26TH MAY

CRUNCH!
THIS PASTA'S A BIT DRY...
CRUNCH!!
STILL...
PASTA SAUCE
PASTA
IT WOULD BE WEIRD EATING PASTA SAUCE ON ITS OWN.
CRUNCH!!

27TH MAY

OOH!
THESE ARE NICE!
SET OFF THE REST OF MY OUTFIT NICELY!
OH YEAH...
THE WASHING UP...

28TH MAY

I LOVE HOOVERING!
IT'S JUST SO LIBERATING!

29TH MAY

ARSES!

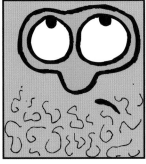

30TH MAY

HMM... MAYBE A TOUCH MORE SALT...
WOOOSH!!
PERFECT!

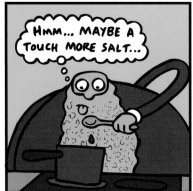

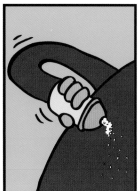

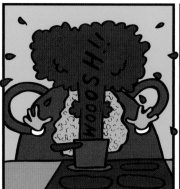

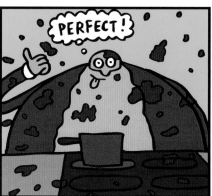

31ST MAY

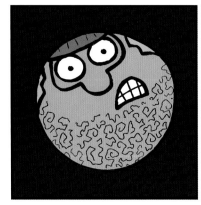

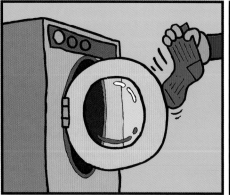

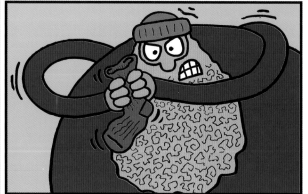

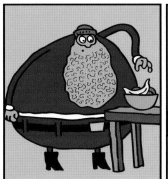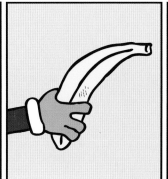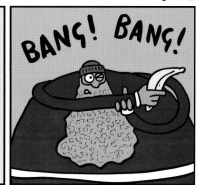

BANG! BANG!

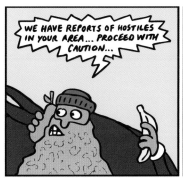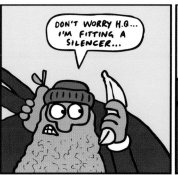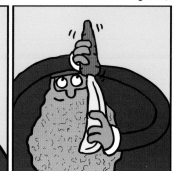

WE HAVE REPORTS OF HOSTILES IN YOUR AREA... PROCEED WITH CAUTION...

DON'T WORRY H.G... I'M FITTING A SILENCER...

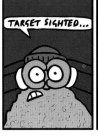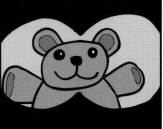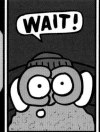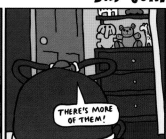

TARGET SIGHTED...

WAIT!

THERE'S MORE OF THEM!

4TH JUNE

HMMM! I'M GOING TO NEED MORE FIRE POWER
LOCK AND LOAD!

5TH JUNE

BLAM!
ACK! ACK! ACK!
DIE TERRORIST SCUM!

6TH JUNE

TELL ME WHERE THE NUCLEAR DEVICE IS!
TALK TO ME GODDAMMIT!
RIGHT... DON'T SAY I DIDN'T WARN YOU...

7TH JUNE

I'VE HAD ENOUGH OF THESE GAMES
BANG!
I JUST WANTED A NAME

8TH JUNE

HUH?
AMBUSH!
BLAM!
BLAM!
CLICK! CLICK!
DAMN! OUT OF AMMO!

9TH JUNE

RIGHT... I'LL TAKE YOU ALL TO HELL WITH ME!
CLICK
AAAAAGGHH!

10TH JUNE

I'M HOME LOVE!
LOVE?
LOVE?
HONESTLY! YOU COULD'VE RUN A HOOVER THROUGH THE PLACE!

11TH JUNE

OK CHAPS... NICE TO SEE YOU ALL LOOKING SO EAGER AND KEEN.
JUST TWO THINGS ON THE AGENDA... FIRST OF ALL THERE'S A NEW MACHINE IN THE CANTEEN...
SELLING CRISPS, NUTS, CHOCOLATE, DRINKS AND ASSORTED SANDWICHES...
AND SECONDLY...
WE'VE ALL BEEN MADE REDUNDANT

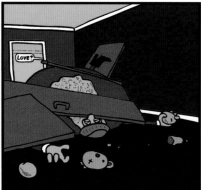

12TH JUNE

THE MOST IMPORTANT THING IS TO NOT FALL INTO BORING CLICHÉS...
I MEAN, JUST BECAUSE WE'RE UNEMPLOYED DOESN'T MEAN WE SHOULD BECOME CRIMINALS...
YOU'RE RIGHT
PRESENTLY...
BASTARD!

13TH JUNE

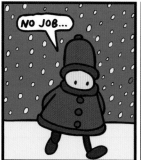
NO JOB...

NO QUALIFICATIONS...

NO PROSPECTS...

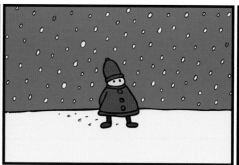

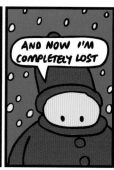
AND NOW I'M COMPLETELY LOST

14TH JUNE

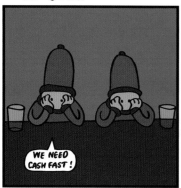
WE NEED CASH FAST!

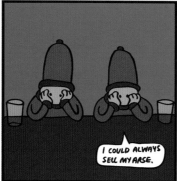
I COULD ALWAYS SELL MY ARSE.

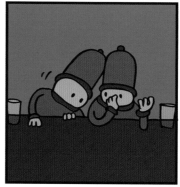

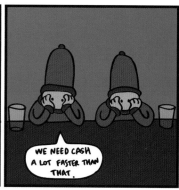
WE NEED CASH A LOT FASTER THAN THAT.

15TH JUNE

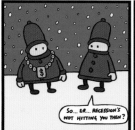
SO... ER... RECESSION'S NOT HITTING YOU THEN?

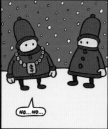
NO... NO...

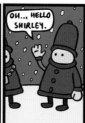
I'M PIMPING OUT THE WIFE AREN'T I?

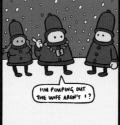
OH... HELLO SHIRLEY.

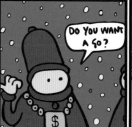
DO YOU WANT A GO?

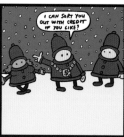
I CAN SORT YOU OUT WITH CREDIT IF YOU LIKE?

16TH JUNE

BIG ISSUE?
ER... NO THANKS
ERM... HOW EXACTLY DID YOU GET IN HERE BY THE WAY?

17TH JUNE

SO HOW DO WE KEEP OUR ECONOMY FROM FALLING FURTHER INTO RECESSION?
IS IT A QUESTION OF GOING TO A 4 DAY WEEK?
OR DO WE TRY TO BOOST THE ECONOMY BY PUMPING IN BILLIONS OF CANDY CANES?
WELL?
HMM... I THINK SACKING EVERYONE WAS PROBABLY A KNEE-JERK REACTION...

18TH JUNE

BEFORE WE START I'D LIKE TO SAY SORRY FOR SACKING YOU ALL...
IT WAS JUST A SILLY MIS-UNDERSTANDING...
I JUST HOPE WE CAN PUT THIS ALL BEHIND US..
OK... SO LET'S GET DOWN TO BUSINESS...
I am a big fat TWAT!

19TH JUNE

OH MY!
I'VE BEEN POKED!
RIGHT! I'LL POKE YOU BACK!
THERE!
I HAVE NO IDEA WHAT ANY OF THAT WAS ABOUT.

20TH JUNE

I'VE BEEN WATCHING TV FOR FIFTEEN HOURS STRAIGHT...
MAYBE I SHOULD GIVE IT A REST...
NO... WAIT...
REMEMBER... WINNERS DON'T QUIT!

21ST JUNE

TODAY THE SUN IS AT ITS HIGHEST POINT.
FROM TOMORROW THE DAYS WILL GET SHORTER...
THEN MAYBE I CAN FINALLY GET SOME SLEEP!

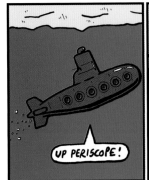

UP PERISCOPE!

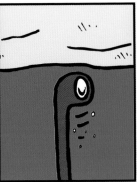

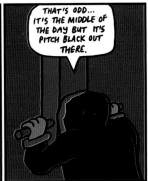

THAT'S ODD...
IT'S THE MIDDLE OF
THE DAY BUT IT'S
PITCH BLACK OUT
THERE.

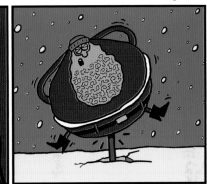

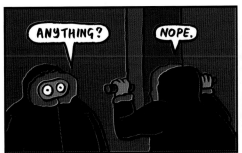

ANYTHING?

NOPE.

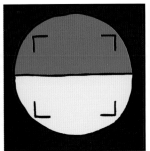

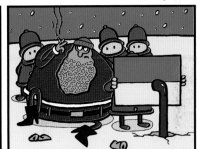

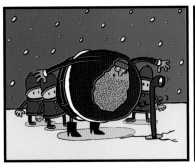

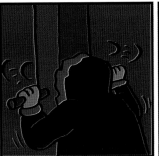

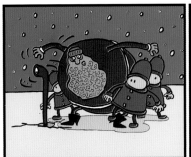

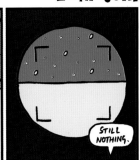

STILL
NOTHING.

25TH JUNE

AS YOU KNOW, WE'VE BEEN HOLDING AUDITIONS TO FIND VIXEN'S REPLACE-MENT...
THINGS ARE GOING OK BUT NONE OF US FEEL WE'VE FOUND 'THE ONE'...
GOOD BOY!
WE'VE DECIDED THE BEST WAY TO CHOOSE IS TO RUN A HUGE RACE, WITH THE RACE WINNER FINDING HIS WAY INTO THE SLEIGH TEAM, AND...
... I'D FORGOTTEN YOU DON'T SPEAK REINDEER.
BLITZEN WANT A SUGAR LUMP?

26TH JUNE

VIXEN REPLACEMENT MARATHON
ON YOUR MARKS... GET SET... GO!!

27TH JUNE

07
24
03
46
46
46
46

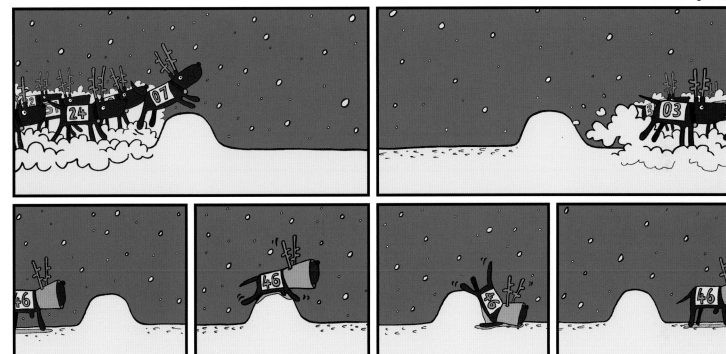

28TH JUNE

46
46
46
46

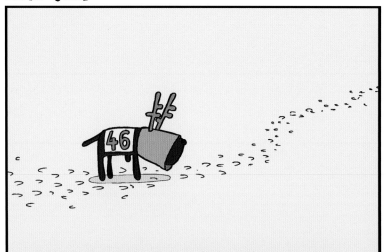

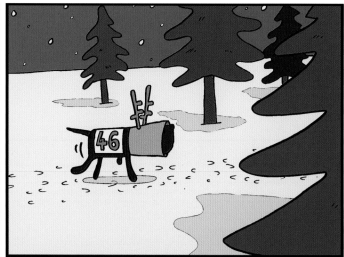

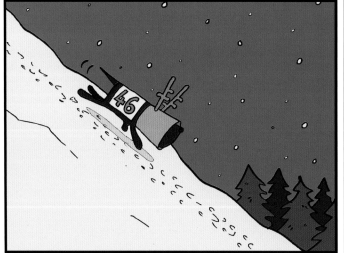

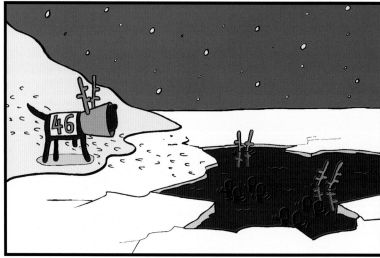

29TH JUNE

WELL TERRY, WE DIDN'T THINK YOU HAD IT IN YOU BUT YOU'VE WON THE RIGHT TO BE VIXEN'S REPLACEMENT...
YOU'VE EARNED OUR RESPECT...
NOW CLEAR AWAY ALL THOSE DEAD BODIES YOU THREE-LEGGED FREAK!
YEAH, FREAK!

30TH JUNE

SO YOU'RE VIXEN'S REPLACEMENT ARE YOU?
GOD HELP US!

1ST JULY

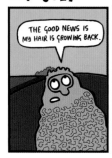

THE GOOD NEWS IS MY HAIR IS GROWING BACK.

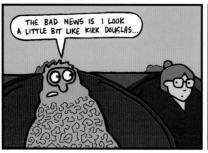

THE BAD NEWS IS I LOOK A LITTLE BIT LIKE KIRK DOUGLAS...

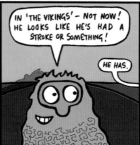

IN 'THE VIKINGS' — NOT NOW! HE LOOKS LIKE HE'S HAD A STROKE OR SOMETHING!

HE HAS.

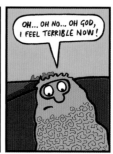

OH... OH NO... OH GOD, I FEEL TERRIBLE NOW!

2ND JULY

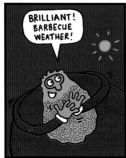

BRILLIANT! BARBECUE WEATHER!

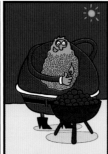

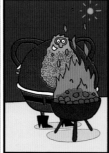

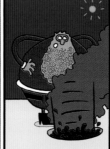

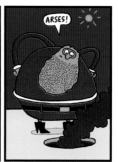

ARSES!

3RD JULY

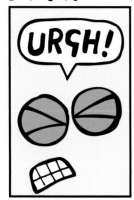

URGH!

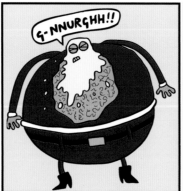

G-NNURGHH!!

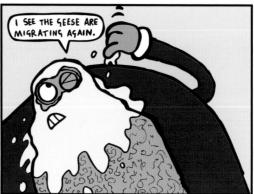

I SEE THE GEESE ARE MIGRATING AGAIN.

4TH JULY

WHEN YOU THINK ABOUT IT IT'S ALL SO POINTLESS ISN'T IT?
WHAT'S POINTLESS?
THIS! US FLYING THOUSANDS OF MILES AT THE START AND END OF THE SUMMER.
GEE I'D NEVER THOUGHT OF IT LIKE THAT BEFORE... I DON'T KNOW WHY WE BOTHER...
STILL, AT LEAST WE'RE NOT GEESE...
YEAH, THERE'S ONE THERE – THE BIG TWAT!

5TH JULY

I'LL GIVE IT ANOTHER MINUTE TO DOWNLOAD...
...TWO AT A PUSH...

6TH JULY

OK... SO...
BROWN IS LIVE...
SO NICE TO FINALLY CLEAR THAT ONE UP.

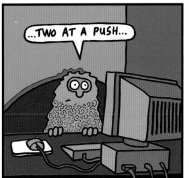

7TH JULY

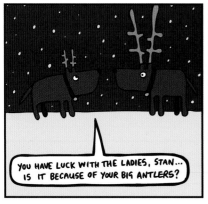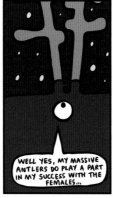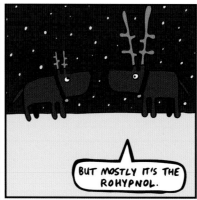

YOU HAVE LUCK WITH THE LADIES, STAN... IS IT BECAUSE OF YOUR BIG ANTLERS?

WELL YES, MY MASSIVE ANTLERS DO PLAY A PART IN MY SUCCESS WITH THE FEMALES...

BUT MOSTLY IT'S THE ROHYPNOL.

8TH JULY

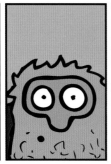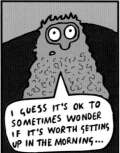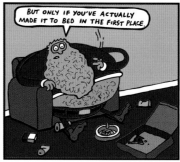

I GUESS IT'S OK TO SOMETIMES WONDER IF IT'S WORTH GETTING UP IN THE MORNING...

BUT ONLY IF YOU'VE ACTUALLY MADE IT TO BED IN THE FIRST PLACE.

9TH JULY

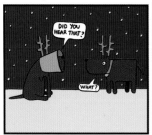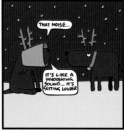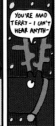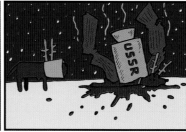

DID YOU HEAR THAT?

WHAT?

THAT NOISE...

IT'S LIKE A WHOOSHING SOUND... IT'S GETTING LOUDER

YOU'RE MAD TERRY - I CAN'T HEAR ANYTH-

USSR

10TH JULY

SO THAT FUNNEL OF YOURS GIVES YOU SUPER HEARING?
I CAN HEAR THAT DASHER AND PRANCER ARE CONTEMPLATING AN AFFAIR...
WOW!
AND I HEARD YOU CALL ME A 'THREE-LEGGED TWAT' FROM WAY OVER THERE.
OH...

11TH JULY

DUCKY & MR. WHALE

THE WATER CERTAINLY IS DEEPER TODAY...
YES.
AND IS IT ME OR IS IT A BIT WARMER TOO?

12TH JULY

ON DASHER, ON DANCER, ON PRANCER, ON BLITZEN! ON COMET, ON CUPID, ON DUNDER, ON TERRY!

13TH JULY

OH MY GOD!
PAY UP OR
I'M TELLING
WHAT U DID
WITH VIXEN

14TH JULY

THIS IS BLACKMAIL!
I think...
DICTIONARY
BLACKMAIL
YES... BLACKMAIL!

15TH JULY

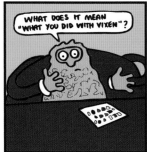

WHAT DOES IT MEAN "WHAT YOU DID WITH VIXEN"?

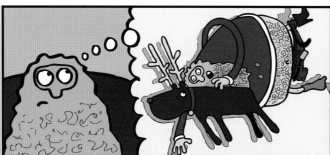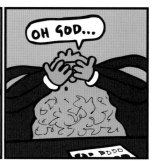

OH GOD...

16TH JULY

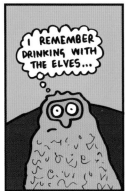

I REMEMBER DRINKING WITH THE ELVES...

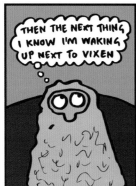

THEN THE NEXT THING I KNOW I'M WAKING UP NEXT TO VIXEN

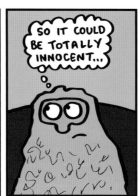

SO IT COULD BE TOTALLY INNOCENT...

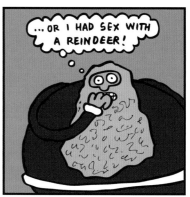

...OR I HAD SEX WITH A REINDEER!

17TH JULY

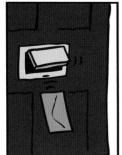

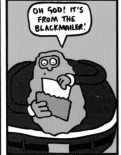

OH GOD! IT'S FROM THE BLACKMAILER!

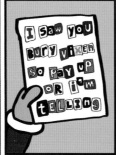

I SAW YOU BURY VIXEN SO PAY UP OR I'M TELLING

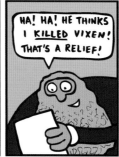

HA! HA! HE THINKS I KILLED VIXEN! THAT'S A RELIEF!

UNLESS OF COURSE 'BURYING VIXEN'S BODY' IS SOME SORT OF EUPHAMISM FOR SORDID ANIMAL BUGGARY!

18TH JULY

LOB!
YEAH...THIS DOES LOOK BAD...

19TH JULY

SO ALL I HAVE TO DO TO PROVE MY INNOCENCE IS FIND WHERE I BURRIED THE BIN BAGS...
I JUST HAVE TO FIND A 2 FOOT HOLE ON THE HUGE, CONSTANTLY SHIFTING POLAR ICE SHEETS...
OH GOD!
I'M BANGED TO RIGHTS!

20TH JULY

THIS IS IT!
LET'S HOPE IT'S 7,314TH TIME LUCKY.

21ST JULY

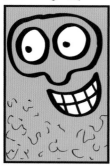

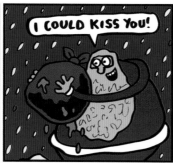

I COULD KISS YOU!

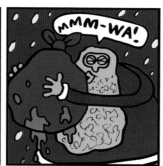

MMM-WA!

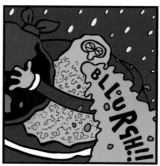

BLLURSH!!!

22ND JULY

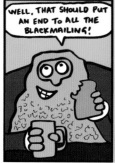

WELL, THAT SHOULD PUT AN END TO ALL THE BLACKMAILING!

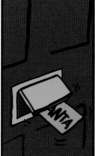

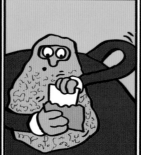

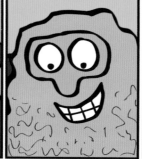

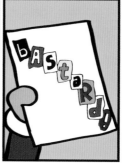

BASTARD!

23RD JULY

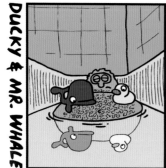

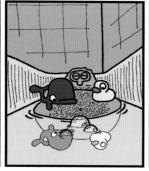

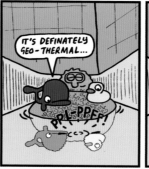

IT'S DEFINATELY GEO-THERMAL...

PRL-PPFF!

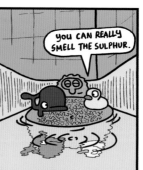

YOU CAN REALLY SMELL THE SULPHUR.

DUCKY & MR. WHALE

24TH JULY

I REALLY MISS VIXEN...
I WONDER WHAT SHE'S UP TO RIGHT NOW...
KEBABS
CHILLI SAUCE?
YEAH, GO ON

25TH JULY

I'D GIVE ANYTHING TO KNOW WHERE VIXEN IS...
SHE'S IN SPAIN.
JUST TO KNOW SHE'S OK...
BARCELONA.
IT'S SO HOPELESS...
YOU HAVE TO LEARN REINDEER YOU IDIOT.

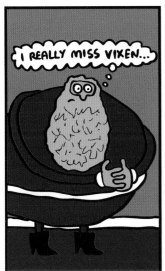

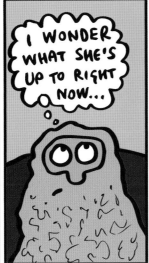

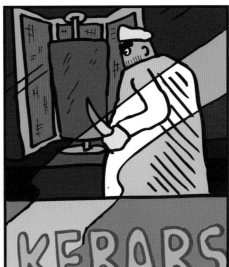

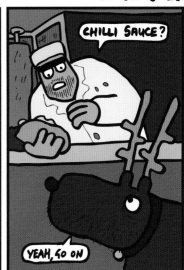

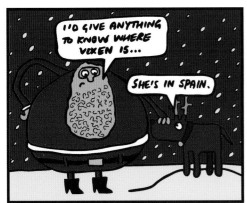

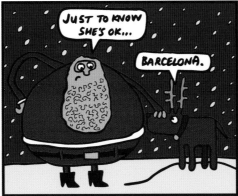

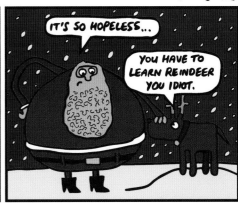

26TH JULY

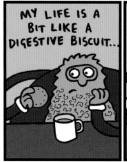
MY LIFE IS A BIT LIKE A DIGESTIVE BISCUIT...

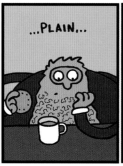
...PLAIN...

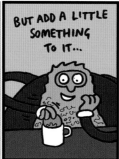
BUT ADD A LITTLE SOMETHING TO IT...

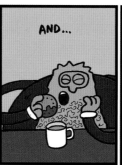
AND...

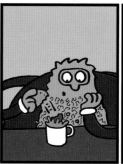

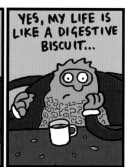
YES, MY LIFE IS LIKE A DIGESTIVE BISCUIT...

27TH JULY

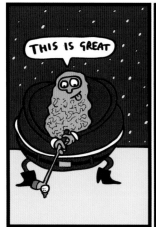
THIS IS GREAT

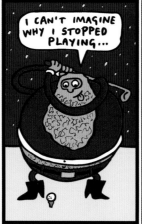
I CAN'T IMAGINE WHY I STOPPED PLAYING...

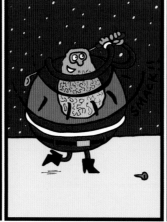
SMACK!!

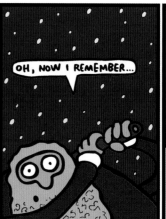
OH, NOW I REMEMBER...

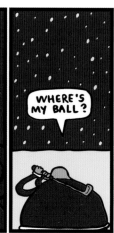
WHERE'S MY BALL?

YAR! YAR! YAR!
UH! UH! UH!
You ALRIGHT LOVE?
HUH! HUH!
UH! UH! UH!
YEAH... ER...
JUST WATCHING THE... ER... DOLPHIN DOCUMENTARY...
ACK-ACK-ACK-ACK-ACK!!!

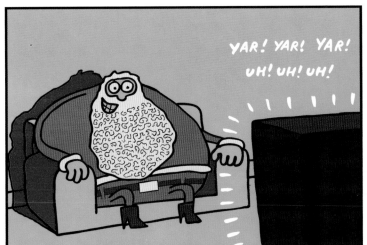

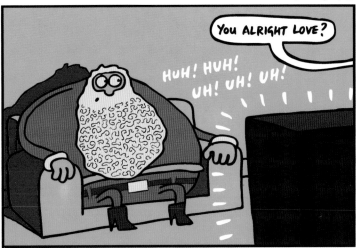

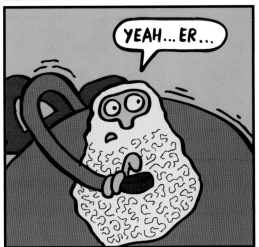

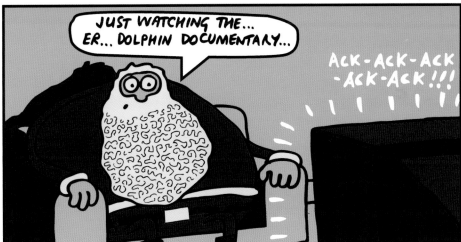

29TH JULY

30TH JULY

HELLO? GUINESS BOOK OF RECORDS? I'VE JUST BALANCED A CHIP ON MY FACE FOR 12 HOURS. IS THAT A RECORD?
OH REALLY...?
27 DAYS...?
OK... WHAT'S THE RECORD NUMBER OF FARTS LIT IN A ROW?

31ST JULY

HiC!!
15 HOURS DRINKING...
BUT I'M HOLDING IT TOGETHER PRETTY WELL.

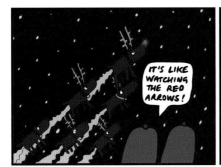

IT'S LIKE
WATCHING
THE RED
ARROWS!

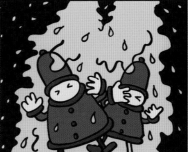

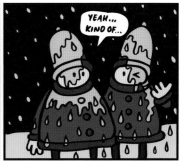

YEAH...
KIND OF...

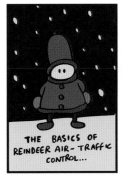

THE BASICS OF
REINDEER AIR-TRAFFIC
CONTROL...

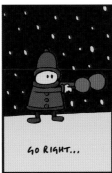

GO RIGHT...

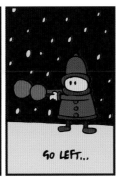

GO LEFT...

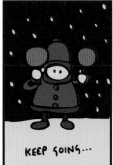

KEEP GOING...

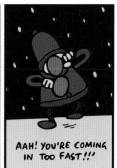

AAH! YOU'RE COMING
IN TOO FAST!!!

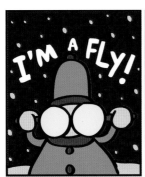

I'M A FLY!

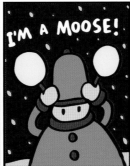

I'M A MOOSE!

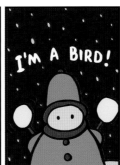

I'M A BIRD!

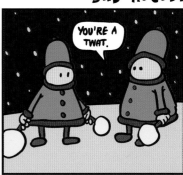

YOU'RE A
TWAT.

4TH AUGUST

OH JUST GO OVER THERE WILL YOU?

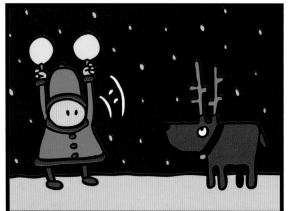

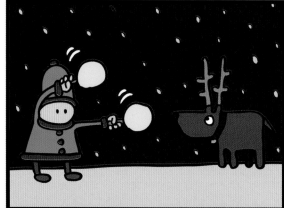

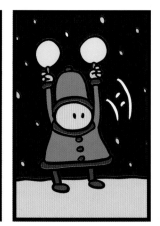

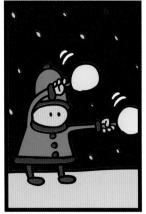

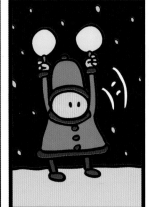

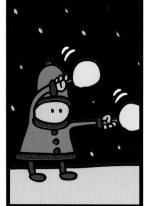

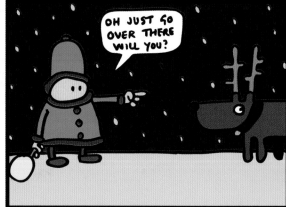

5TH AUGUST

WHAT'S HE SAYING?
DOESN'T ACTUALLY MAKE ANY SENSE...
SOMETHING ABOUT POLAD BEADS?
GRRRR!!
OH HANG ON... THAT'S 'R' ISN'T IT?

6TH AUGUST

WOULD YOU LOVE ME MORE IF I HAD A BIG FUNNEL THING?
NOT REALLY...
I JUST WISH YOU HAD A BIGGER COCK.

7TH AUGUST

LA! LA! LA! TAKING OUT THE BINS!
CRACK!
ARSES!

8TH AUGUST

STUCK HERE LIKE THIS I'M AT THE MERCY OF THE ELEMENTS, POLAR BEARS... AND...
AARGHH!
Y-URGH-HH!!
BIN JUICE!!

9TH AUGUST

GO ON! HAVE A BITE!
SNIFF! SNIFF!
URGH!!!
SMELLS OFF!

10TH AUGUST

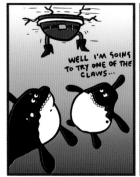
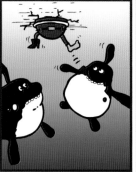
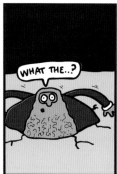
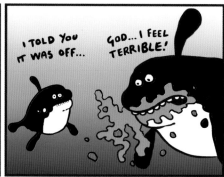

11TH AUGUST

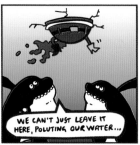
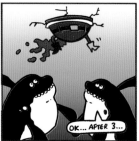
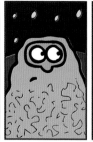
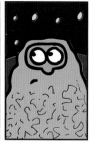
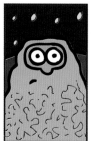
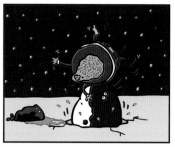

12TH AUGUST

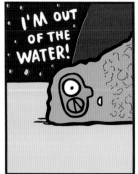
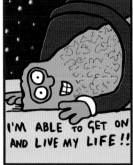
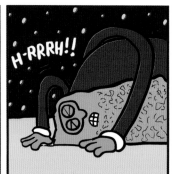
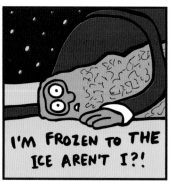

13TH AUGUST

URGH!
BLURGH!
OH COME ON! GIVE US A BREAK!!

14TH AUGUST

H-URRGHH!!
G-N-AARH!!
Y-ESSS!!
W-OOAH!!

15TH AUGUST

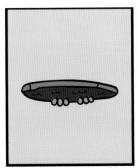

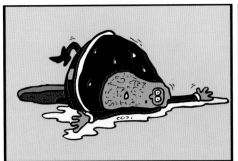

16TH AUGUST

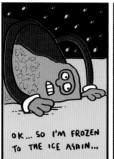
OK... SO I'M FROZEN TO THE ICE AGAIN...

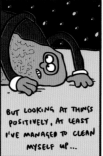
BUT LOOKING AT THINGS POSITIVELY, AT LEAST I'VE MANAGED TO CLEAN MYSELF UP...

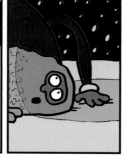

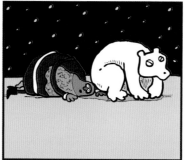

17TH AUGUST

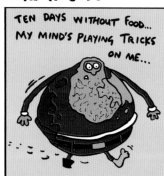
TEN DAYS WITHOUT FOOD... MY MIND'S PLAYING TRICKS ON ME...

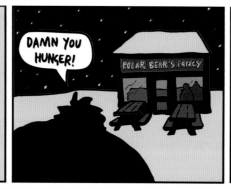
DAMN YOU HUNGER!

POLAR BEAR'S FANCY

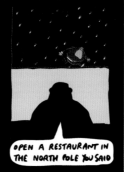
OPEN A RESTAURANT IN THE NORTH POLE YOU SAID

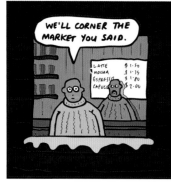
WE'LL CORNER THE MARKET YOU SAID.

LATTE $1·50
MOCHA $1·75
ESPRESSO $1·80
CAPUCC... $2·00

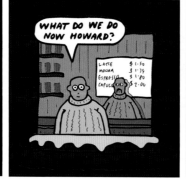
WHAT DO WE DO NOW HOWARD?

LATTE $1·50
MOCHA $1·75
ESPRESSO $1·80
CAPUCC... $2·00

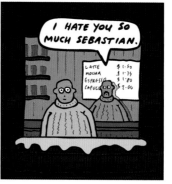
I HATE YOU SO MUCH SEBASTIAN.

LATTE $1·50
MOCHA $1·75
ESPRESSO $1·80
CAPUCC... $2·00

18TH AUGUST

AH! THERE YOU ARE!
JUST IN TIME TO TAKE THE BINS OUT.

19TH AUGUST

THIS IS INTERESTING...
...FASCINATING...
... MY EYES ARE READING BUT MY BRAIN IS TAKING ABSOLUTELY NOTHING IN.

20TH AUGUST

DRIP! DRIP!
HMM... WELL I HAVEN'T PISSED MYSELF THIS TIME...
DRIP! DRIP! DRIP!
I BETTER GET UP AND HAVE A LOOK...
HMFPH!

21ST AUGUST

BRILLIANT! THE ENTIRE HOUSE IS RUINED THANKS TO A LEAKY PIPE.
AND NOW IT'S FROZEN.

22ND AUGUST

OK, SO IT'S 25 TO CLEAR MY GUTTERS OF LEAVES...
...AND 50 TO CLEAR DEAD BIRDS...
HOW MUCH FOR HUMANS?

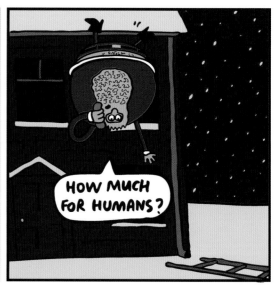

23RD AUGUST

AH! MY TRUSTY OLD TOOL BOX!
I JUST NEED A CUTTING TOOL TO GET THIS OLD PADLOCK OFF...
TOOLS
TOOLS
TOOLS

24TH AUGUST

IT'S A BIT RUSTY BUT I'M SURE IT'S STILL OK...

25TH AUGUST

HMM... NOT SURE IT'S THE RIGHT TOOL...
AH... NOW THIS IS MORE LIKE IT!
CLANK!

26TH AUGUST

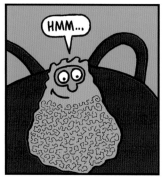

HMM...

IS THERE ANYTHING MORE SATISFYING...

THAN A JOB WELL DONE?

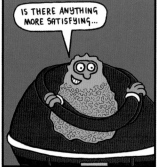

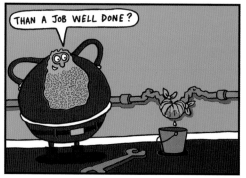

27TH AUGUST

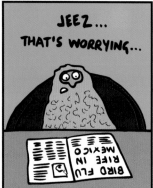

JEEZ...
THAT'S WORRYING...

BIRD FLU RIFE IN MEXICO

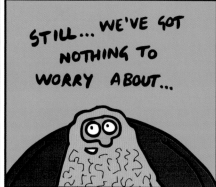

STILL... WE'VE GOT NOTHING TO WORRY ABOUT...

NO ONE WE KNOW HAS BEEN TO MEXICO...

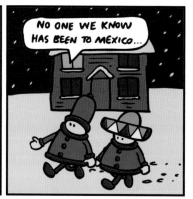

28TH AUGUST

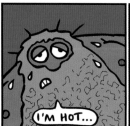

I'M HOT...

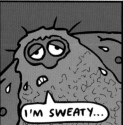

I'M SWEATY...

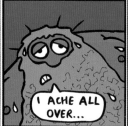

I ACHE ALL OVER...

IT'S OK DEAR, WE CAN TRY AGAIN NEXT YEAR.

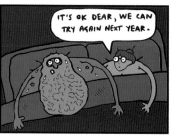

29TH AUGUST

HELLO? THANKS FOR WAITING... HELLO? HELLO?

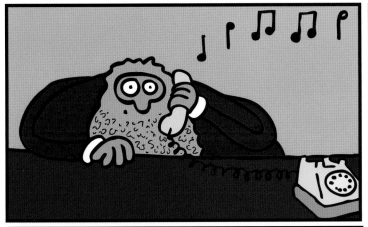

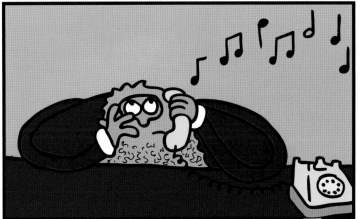

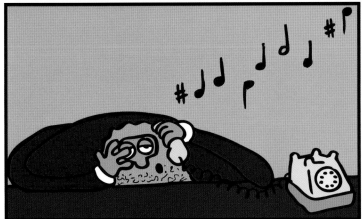

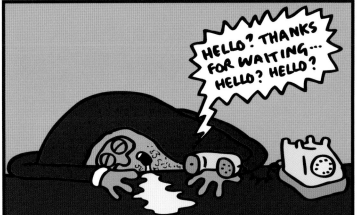

30TH AUGUST

THE MALE TIGER CHOOSES HIS FEMALE AND THEN MOUNTS HER...
ROAR!
ROAR!
I'VE BEEN WATCHING TV TOO LONG...
RROARR!
ROAR!
THIS IS VAGUELY AROUSING!
RRROARRR!!
R-R-ROOARR!!
RROARRR!!

31ST AUGUST

I WAS A BIT BORED SO I MILKED THE REINDEER...
DIDN'T GET MUCH OUT OF THEM BUT THEY SEEMED HAPPY.
SOME OF THEM QUEUED UP TWICE.

1ST SEPTEMBER

MUST SCRUB AWAY STENCH OF EMBARRASSMENT
...AND...
REINDEER WILLY

2ND SEPTEMBER

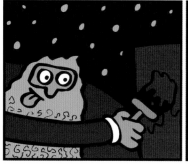
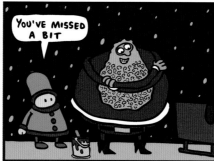
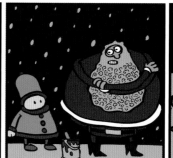
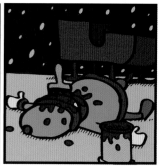

3RD SEPTEMBER

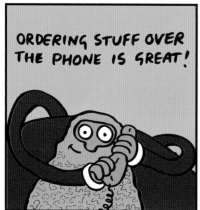
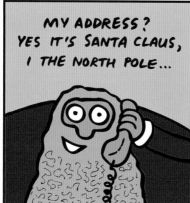
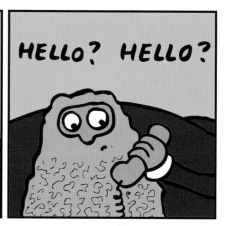

4TH SEPTEMBER

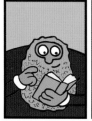
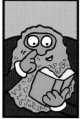
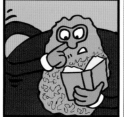
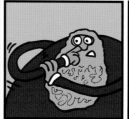
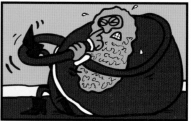

5TH SEPTEMBER

WHAT IS THAT?
LOOKS LIKE SOME SORT OF PLANE, BUT IT'S TOO FAR AWAY TO MAKE OUT PROP-
OW!

6TH SEPTEMBER

AAGHH! RESTLESS LEG!!

7TH SEPTEMBER

43
WE INTERUPT THE SNOOKER TO BRING YOU THIS IMPORTANT NEWS FLASH...
74 DEAD IN SRI LANKA...
WELCOME BACK TO THE SNOOKER

8TH SEPTEMBER

I FEEL TERRIBLE!
I DON'T THINK ANYONE IN THE WORLD COULD FEEL AS BAD AS ME
NO OFFENSE, STUMPY
NONE TAKEN

9TH SEPTEMBER

10TH SEPTEMBER

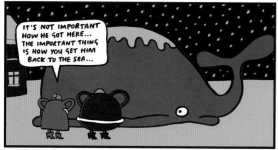

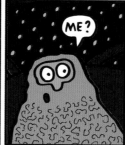

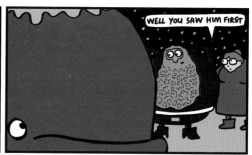

11TH SEPTEMBER

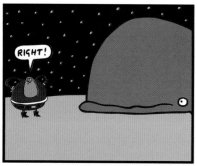

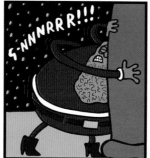

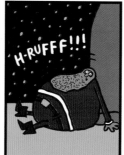

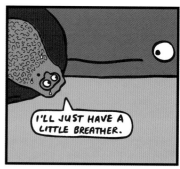

12TH SEPTEMBER

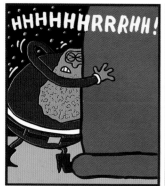

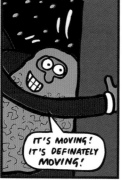

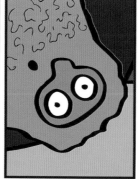

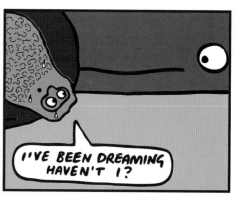

13TH SEPTEMBER

14TH SEPTEMBER

AT LAST! WE'RE MOVING!
THAT'S ODD...

15TH SEPTEMBER

16TH SEPTEMBER

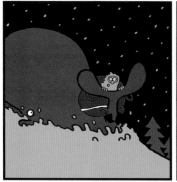 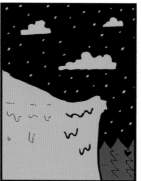 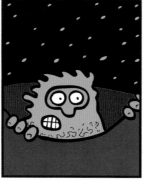 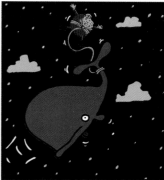

17TH SEPTEMBER

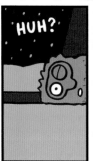 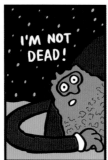 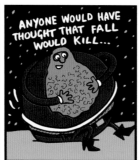 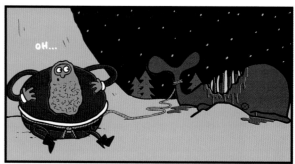

18TH SEPTEMBER

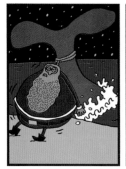 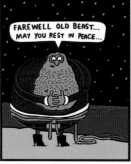 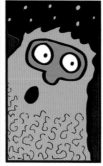 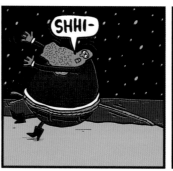 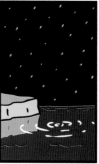

19TH SEPTEMBER
20TH SEPTEMBER
G-RRRRRR!!!
FOR THE LAST TIME...
I AM NOT YOUR LEADER!
21ST SEPTEMBER
JEEZ, I DON'T KNOW WHICH IS MORE EMBARRASSING...
BEING MISTAKEN FOR AN ELEPHANT SEAL OR THE FACT I CAN'T OUT RUN THEM...

22ND SEPTEMBER

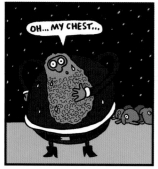

OH... MY CHEST...

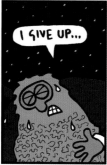

I GIVE UP...

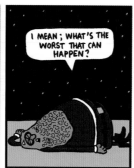

I MEAN; WHAT'S THE WORST THAT CAN HAPPEN?

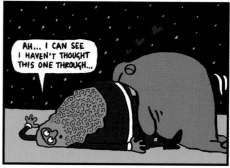

AH... I CAN SEE I HAVEN'T THOUGHT THIS ONE THROUGH...

23RD SEPTEMBER

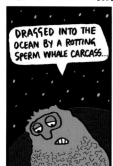

DRAGGED INTO THE OCEAN BY A ROTTING SPERM WHALE CARCASS...

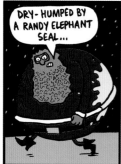

DRY-HUMPED BY A RANDY ELEPHANT SEAL...

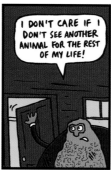

I DON'T CARE IF I DON'T SEE ANOTHER ANIMAL FOR THE REST OF MY LIFE!

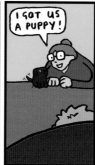

I GOT US A PUPPY!

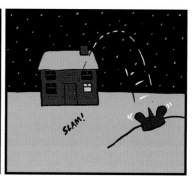

SLAM!

24TH SEPTEMBER

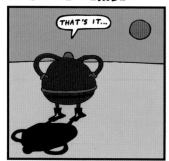

THAT'S IT...

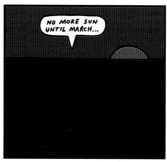

NO MORE SUN UNTIL MARCH...

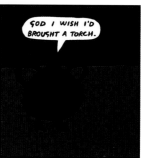

GOD I WISH I'D BROUGHT A TORCH.

25TH SEPTEMBER

THANK GOD IT'S A FULL MOON.
ARSES.

26TH SEPTEMBER

OH NO! A BLACKOUT!
QUICK! FIND A TORCH!
DON'T LOOK AT ME I'M AN ARCTIC HARE.

27TH SEPTEMBER

IT'S SO DARK I CAN'T SEE MY HAND THAT'S TOUCHING MY FACE.
YOUR HAND ISN'T TOUCHING YOUR FACE.
IT'S NOT EVEN TOUCHING MY FACE.

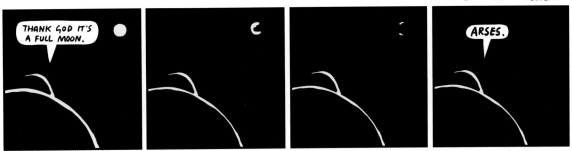

28TH SEPTEMBER

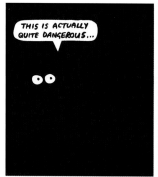

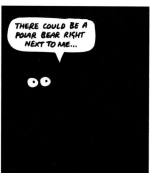

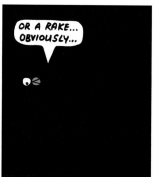

29TH SEPTEMBER

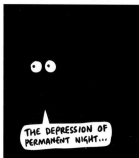

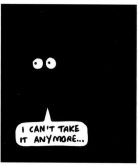

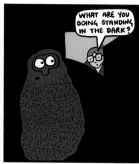

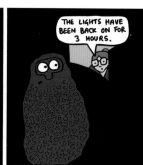

30TH SEPTEMBER

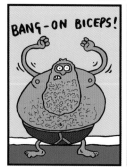

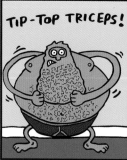

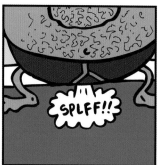

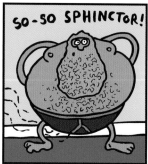

1ST OCTOBER

OOH!
WOW, THAT DREAM WAS VIVID!

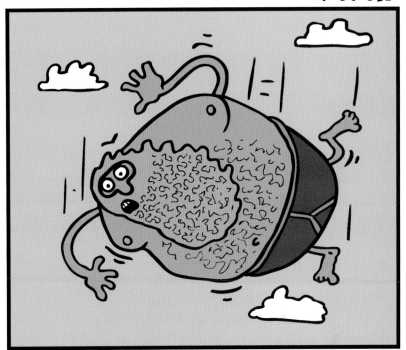

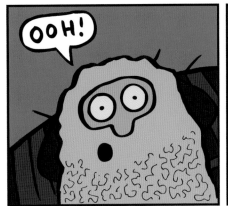

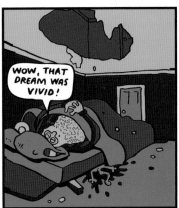

2ND OCTOBER

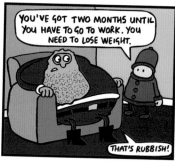

YOU'VE GOT TWO MONTHS UNTIL YOU HAVE TO GO TO WORK. YOU NEED TO LOSE WEIGHT.

THAT'S RUBBISH!

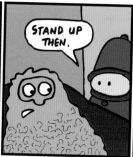

STAND UP THEN.

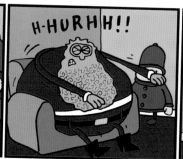

H-HURHH!!

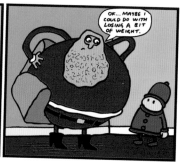

OK... MAYBE I COULD DO WITH LOSING A BIT OF WEIGHT.

3RD OCTOBER

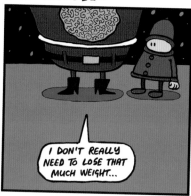

I DON'T REALLY NEED TO LOSE THAT MUCH WEIGHT...

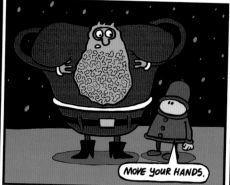

MOVE YOUR HANDS.

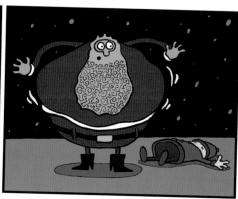

4TH OCTOBER

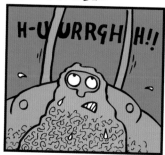

H-UURRGHH!!

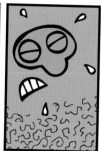

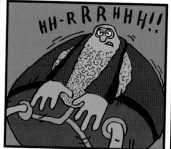

HH-RRRHHH!!

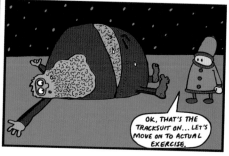

OK, THAT'S THE TRACKSUIT ON... LET'S MOVE ON TO ACTUAL EXERCISE.

5TH OCTOBER

AAAGH! STITCH!!

6TH OCTOBER

I'VE MADE THIS SO WE KNOW WHEN YOU'VE LOST ENOUGH WEIGHT.
IT'S BASED ON THE AVERAGE SIZE OF A CHIMNEY.
WOW! THAT'S DEPRESSING.

7TH OCTOBER

TOO SLOW.

8TH OCTOBER

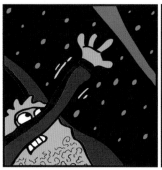 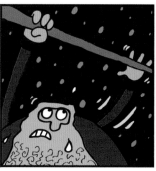 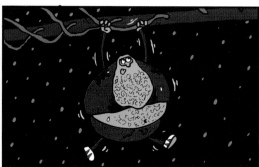

9TH OCTOBER

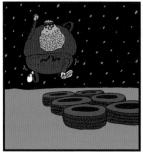 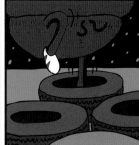 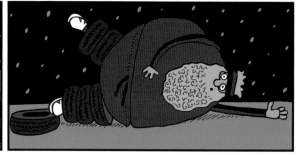

10TH OCTOBER

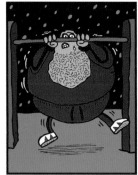 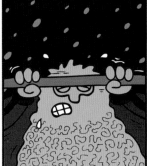 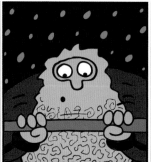 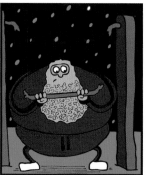

11TH OCTOBER

STROKE! STROKE!
HANG ON A SECOND... WHY AM I EXERCISING?
STROKE!!
I'M SANTA! I CAN MAGIC MYSELF DOWN CHIMNEYS!
AH...
I GUESS I ASKED FOR THAT.

12TH OCTOBER

DUCKY & MR. WHALE
CAN YOU ACTUALLY BLOW OUT OF YOUR BLOW HOLE?
I DON'T KNOW... I'LL GIVE IT A GO...
HH-RHH!!
GRR-HHH!!!
I GUESS NOT.

13TH OCTOBER

DUCKY & MR. WHALE
DO YOU EVER LONG FOR ADVENTURE?
TO FLOAT WHERE THE OCEAN CURRENTS TAKE YOU?
BE AT THE WHIM OF THIS AWE-INSPIRING WORLD?
NO, NOT REALLY.
YEAH ME NEITHER.

14TH OCTOBER

BRILLIANT! IT'S ARRIVED!
WHAT IS IT?
MOBILITY SKIDDOO...
AND WHEN ARE YOU GOING TO USE THAT?
ALL THE TIME!

15TH OCTOBER

SO... WHERE ARE YOU GOING ON YOUR FIRST EXPEDITION?
THE ARCTIC MOUNTAINS? THE GREAT POLAR ICE SHEETS?
NOPE!
THE TOILET!
ERRRRRRRR!!!

16TH OCTOBER

HELLO REINDEER!
HELLO POLAR BEARS!
HI SEALS!
ARSES!

17TH OCTOBER

CUP OF TEA?
IT'S OK, I'LL GET IT...
NO! WAIT!
RRRRERRR!!!!
ONE LUMP OR TWO?

18TH OCTOBER

YOU'VE GONE TOO FAR WITH THIS YOU KNOW?
NOW YOU'RE JUST BEING CRIPPLE-IST!
YOU CAN'T SAY CRIPPLE!!
SAYS YOU AND YOUR FASCIST, NON-CRIPPLE-IST WORLD.

19TH OCTOBER

WHAT ARE YOU UP TO?
I WAS JUST THINKING THAT IF I CUT A HOLE IN THE SKIDDOO AND GET SHOT OF THE TOILET...
I COULD GO TO THE LOO WITHOUT EVER GETTING OFF!

20TH OCTOBER

NICE DAY!
LOVELY
EEERRRRRRRR!!
WE'VE GOT TO GET HIM OFF THAT THING!

21ST OCTOBER

HA! HA! HA! HA!
HUH?
DAMN MY DYSLEXIA!
Satan

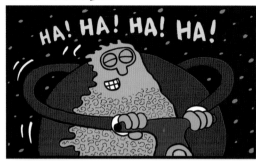

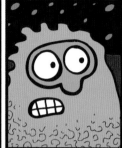

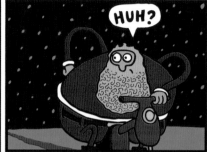

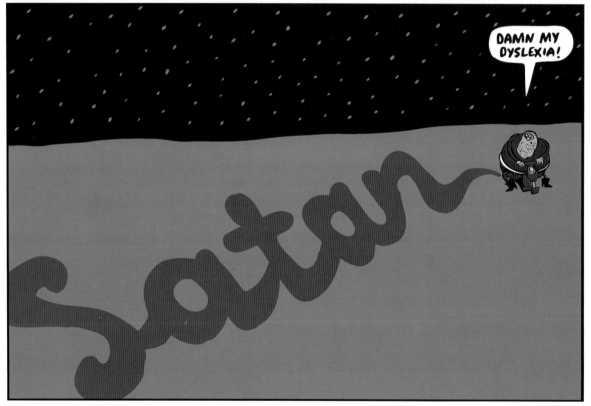

22ND OCTOBER

ISN'T THE NOVELTY WEARING OFF YET?
NO.

23RD OCTOBER

YOU KNOW WHAT WOULD BE GOOD TO DO ON THAT THING?
WHAT?
JUMP THE GORGE!
YEAH!

24TH OCTOBER

YOU DON'T HAVE TO GO THROUGH WITH THIS YOU KNOW?
NO CHANCE!
I DIDN'T SPEND 3 HOURS GETTING INTO THIS OUTFIT FOR NOTHING!

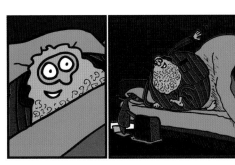

25TH OCTOBER

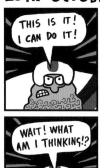

THIS IS IT!
I CAN DO IT!

WAIT! WHAT
AM I THINKING!?

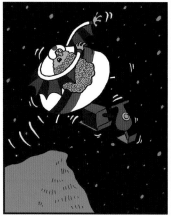

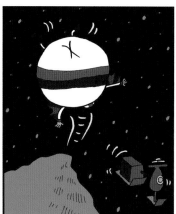

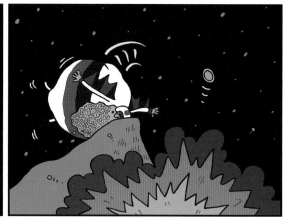

26TH OCTOBER

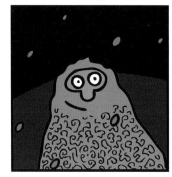

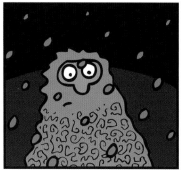

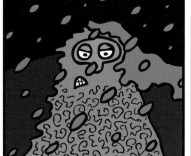

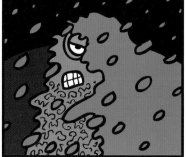

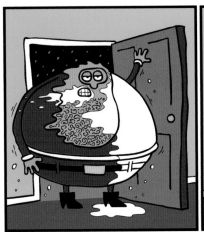
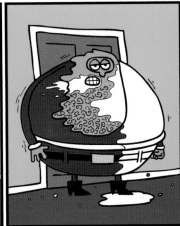
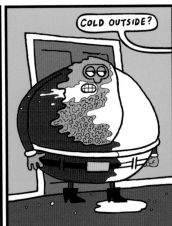
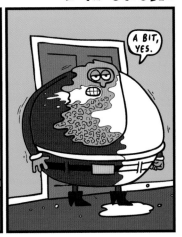

COLD OUTSIDE?

A BIT, YES.

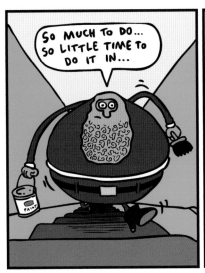
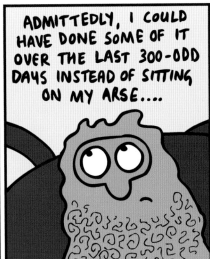
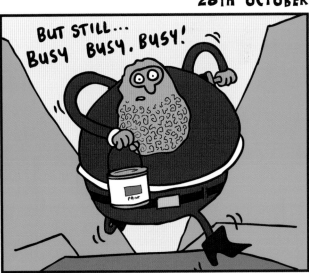

SO MUCH TO DO... SO LITTLE TIME TO DO IT IN...

ADMITTEDLY, I COULD HAVE DONE SOME OF IT OVER THE LAST 300-ODD DAYS INSTEAD OF SITTING ON MY ARSE....

BUT STILL... BUSY BUSY. BUSY!

29TH OCTOBER

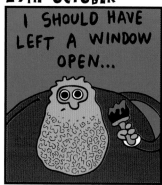

I SHOULD HAVE LEFT A WINDOW OPEN...

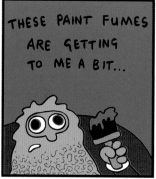

THESE PAINT FUMES ARE GETTING TO ME A BIT...

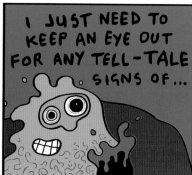

I JUST NEED TO KEEP AN EYE OUT FOR ANY TELL-TALE SIGNS OF...

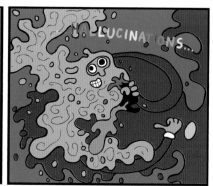

HALLUCINATIONS...

30TH OCTOBER

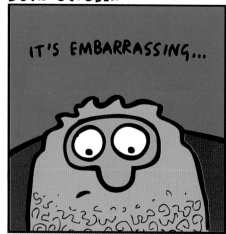

IT'S EMBARRASSING...

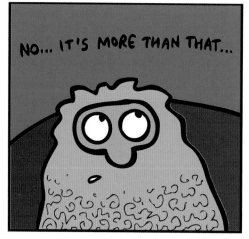

NO... IT'S MORE THAN THAT...

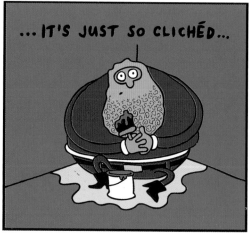

...IT'S JUST SO CLICHÉD...

31ST OCTOBER

HMMF!
IT'S A FINE LINE ISN'T IT?
... BETWEEN JOLLY...
...AND MORBIDLY OBESE.

1ST NOVEMBER

AAGH!!
MY KEYS!

2ND NOVEMBER

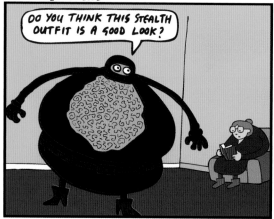

DO YOU THINK THIS STEALTH OUTFIT IS A GOOD LOOK?

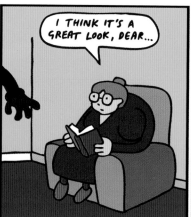

I THINK IT'S A GREAT LOOK, DEAR...

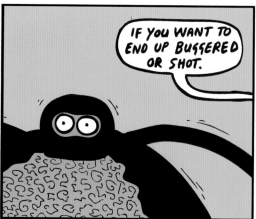

IF YOU WANT TO END UP BUGGERED OR SHOT.

3RD NOVEMBER

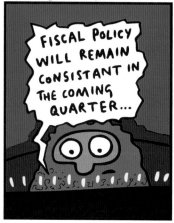

FISCAL POLICY WILL REMAIN CONSISTANT IN THE COMING QUARTER...

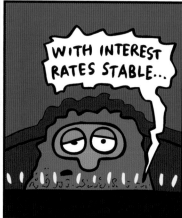

WITH INTEREST RATES STABLE...

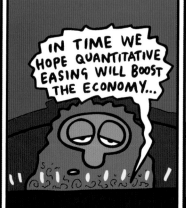

IN TIME WE HOPE QUANTITATIVE EASING WILL BOOST THE ECONOMY...

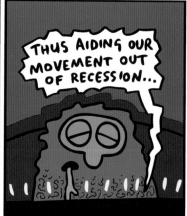

THUS AIDING OUR MOVEMENT OUT OF RECESSION...

4TH NOVEMBER

HAVING A FALL IS A DEPRESSING REMINDER OF OUR FRAILTY AND OLD AGE...
BUT ON THE PLUS SIDE...
I DIDN'T SPILL A DROP OF MY DRINK!

5TH NOVEMBER

SO MANY QUESTIONS...
ARE WE ALONE IN THE UNIVERSE?
WILL WE EVER FIND INTELLIGENT LIFE OUT THERE?
HAVE I ACTUALLY BROKEN MY SPINE, OR WILL THE FEELING RETURN TO MY LEGS SOON?

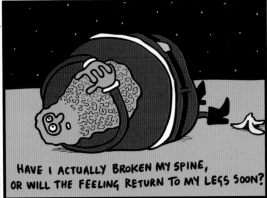

6TH NOVEMBER

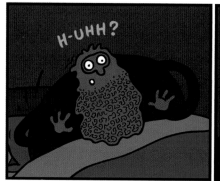

H-UHH?

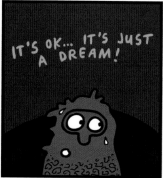

IT'S OK... IT'S JUST A DREAM!

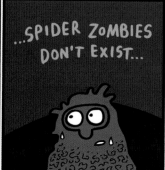

...SPIDER ZOMBIES DON'T EXIST...

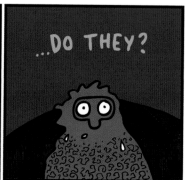

...DO THEY?

7TH NOVEMBER

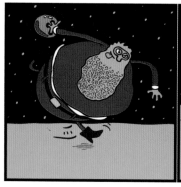

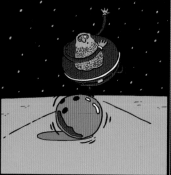

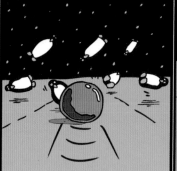

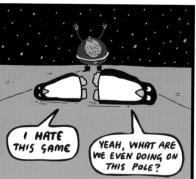

I HATE THIS GAME

YEAH, WHAT ARE WE EVEN DOING ON THIS POLE?

8TH NOVEMBER

I LOVE BEING SANTA...
I'M NEVER, EVER FAT; I'M JOLLY!
HEE! HEE! LOOK! HOW JOLLY I AM!

9TH NOVEMBER

SHIT!
NO, ACTUALLY IT'S CHOCOLATE!

10TH NOVEMBER

45 DAYS TO CHRISTMAS!
THIS IS IT! TIME TO GET TO WORK! SO IF YOU'RE NOT UP FOR THE CHALLENGE I SUGGEST YOU LEAVE NOW.

11TH NOVEMBER

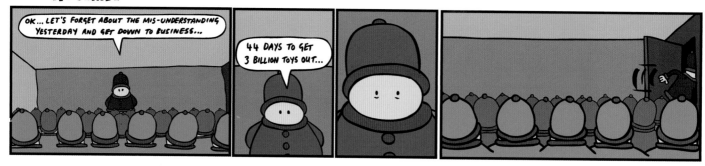

12TH NOVEMBER

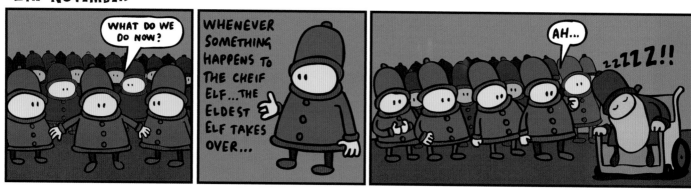

13TH NOVEMBER

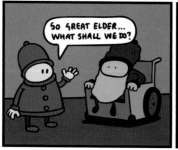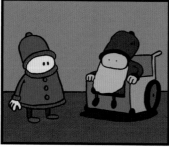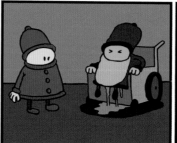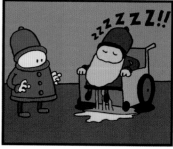

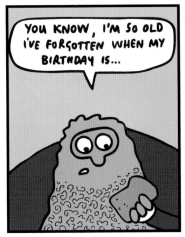

YOU KNOW, I'M SO OLD I'VE FORGOTTEN WHEN MY BIRTHDAY IS...

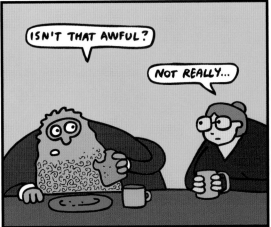

ISN'T THAT AWFUL?

NOT REALLY...

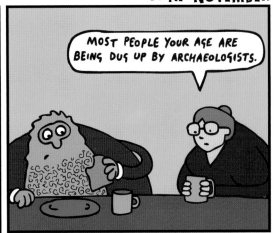

MOST PEOPLE YOUR AGE ARE BEING DUG UP BY ARCHAEOLOGISTS.

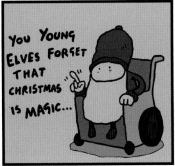

YOU YOUNG ELVES FORGET THAT CHRISTMAS IS MAGIC...

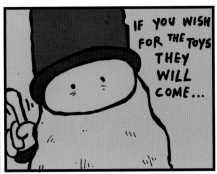

IF YOU WISH FOR THE TOYS THEY WILL COME...

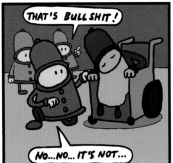

THAT'S BULLSHIT!

NO...NO... IT'S NOT...

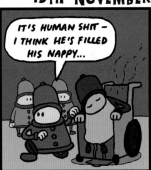

IT'S HUMAN SHIT – I THINK HE'S FILLED HIS NAPPY...

16TH NOVEMBER

ANYTHING?
NOPE.
I THINK I'VE POPPED OUT ANOTHER PILE.

17TH NOVEMBER

YOU KNOW, I THINK THE OLD MAN WAS WRONG...
I THINK HE WAS TALKING OUT OF HIS AR-
GH!

18TH NOVEMBER

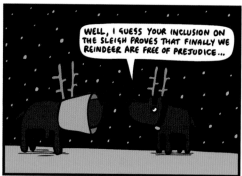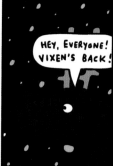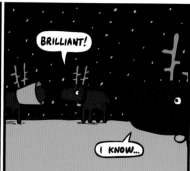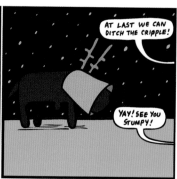

WELL, I GUESS YOUR INCLUSION ON THE SLEIGH PROVES THAT FINALLY WE REINDEER ARE FREE OF PREJUDICE...

HEY, EVERYONE! VIXEN'S BACK!

BRILLIANT!

I KNOW...

AT LAST WE CAN DITCH THE CRIPPLE!

YAY! SEE YOU STUMPY!

19TH NOVEMBER

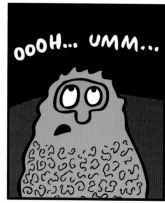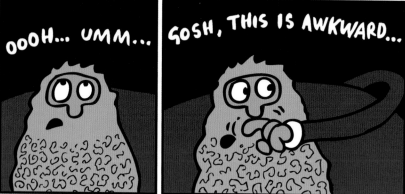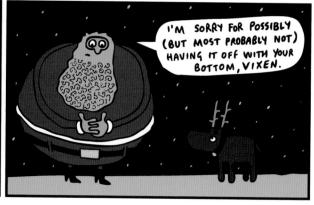

OOOH... UMM...

GOSH, THIS IS AWKWARD...

I'M SORRY FOR POSSIBLY (BUT MOST PROBABLY NOT) HAVING IT OFF WITH YOUR BOTTOM, VIXEN.

20TH NOVEMBER

YOU KNOW, SOMETIMES I LONG FOR THE OLD DAYS
WHEN WE SPENT ALL YEAR IN WORKSHOPS...
... CRAFTING TOYS WITH LOVE...
THEN I REMEMBER HOW DULL IT WAS AND I GO BACK TO LONGING FOR A PINT AND A HAND JOB.

21ST NOVEMBER

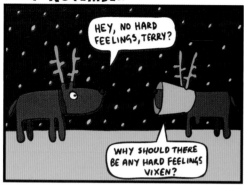

HEY, NO HARD FEELINGS, TERRY?

WHY SHOULD THERE BE ANY HARD FEELINGS VIXEN?

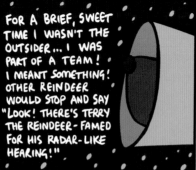

FOR A BRIEF, SWEET TIME I WASN'T THE OUTSIDER... I WAS PART OF A TEAM! I MEANT SOMETHING! OTHER REINDEER WOULD STOP AND SAY "LOOK! THERE'S TERRY THE REINDEER-FAMED FOR HIS RADAR-LIKE HEARING!"

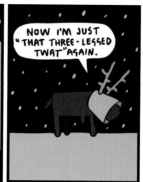

NOW I'M JUST "THAT THREE-LEGGED TWAT" AGAIN.

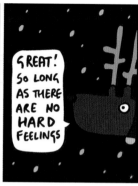

GREAT! SO LONG AS THERE ARE NO HARD FEELINGS

22ND NOVEMBER

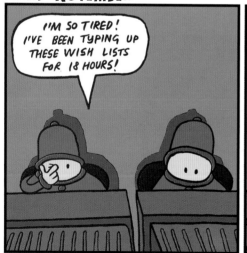

I'M SO TIRED! I'VE BEEN TYPING UP THESE WISH LISTS FOR 18 HOURS!

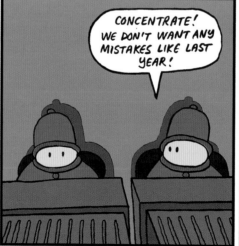

CONCENTRATE! WE DON'T WANT ANY MISTAKES LIKE LAST YEAR!

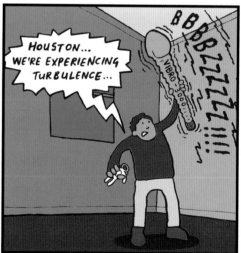

HOUSTON... WE'RE EXPERIENCING TURBULENCE...

VIBRO 3000

BBBBZZZZZZ!!!!

23RD NOVEMBER

I'VE FOUND A DEAD CAT IN ONE OF THE CONTAINERS.
OH... ERM...
TELL YOU WHAT, JUST WRAP IT UP AND WE'LL SEND IT TO ONE OF THE NAUGHTY KIDS.

24TH NOVEMBER

THAT'S THE NICE LIST THERE...
AND THIS IS THE NAUGHTY LIST.

25TH NOVEMBER

AREN'T YOU JEALOUS YOU'RE NOT ON THE SLEIGH TEAM?
IT'S NOT REALLY JEALOUSY...
I'D JUST LIKE THEM ALL TO DIE IN A FIRE BALL OVER THE SEA AND THEN BE EATEN BY INSECTOID AQUATIC PARASITES.
SERIOUSLY... YOU NEED HELP.

26TH NOVEMBER

I'VE PROGRAMMED ALL THE DESTINATIONS YOU NEED INTO THIS SAT NAV...
THINK OF IT AS INSURANCE...
IN CASE SOMETHING HAPPENS TO RUDOLF.
WE'RE WORRIED ABOUT TERRY.

27TH NOVEMBER

MUST REMEMBER TO MAKE THE REINDEER GO TO THE TOILET BEFORE I TAKE THE SLEIGH UP.

28TH NOVEMBER

CAREFUL!
EASY DOES IT!
WATCH IT!
SORRY

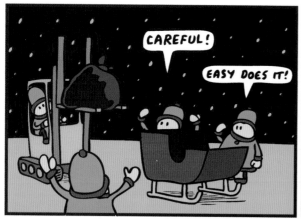

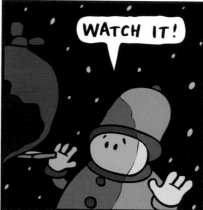

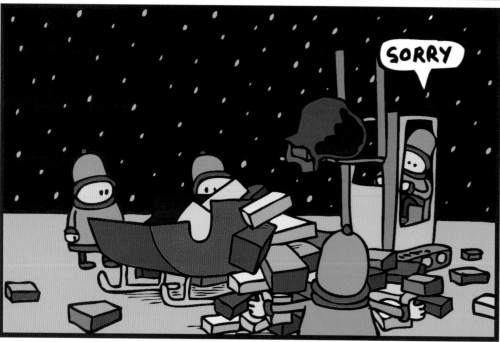

29TH NOVEMBER

IT'S AMAZING ISN'T IT?
DON'T THINK ABOUT IT
300 CONTAINERS OF TOYS IN ONE SACK - IT'S CRAZY!
HONESTLY - IT'S BEST TO JUST IGNORE IT...
MY MIND'S STRAINING AT THE QUANTUM PHYSICS INVOLVED...
PAFF!
I TOLD YOU NOT TO THINK ABOUT IT!

30TH NOVEMBER

H-RMPH!!
I BET JESUS DOESN'T HAVE TO WRITE CHRISTMAS CARDS!

DUCKY & MR. WHALE

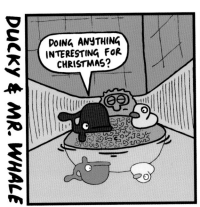

DOING ANYTHING INTERESTING FOR CHRISTMAS?

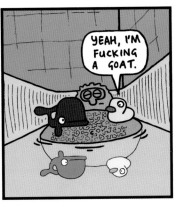

YEAH, I'M FUCKING A GOAT.

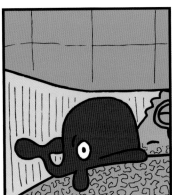

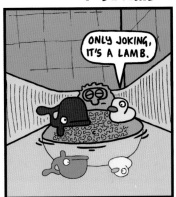

ONLY JOKING, IT'S A LAMB.

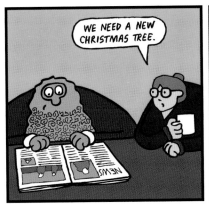

WE NEED A NEW CHRISTMAS TREE.

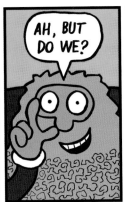

AH, BUT DO WE?

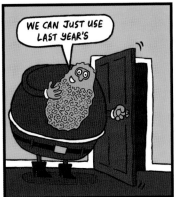

WE CAN JUST USE LAST YEAR'S

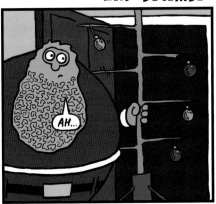

AH...

3RD DECEMBER

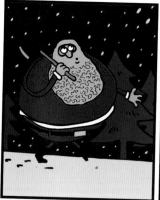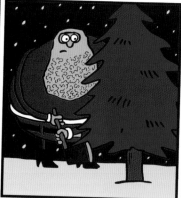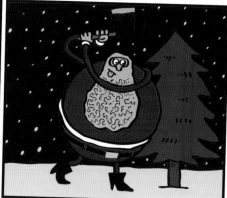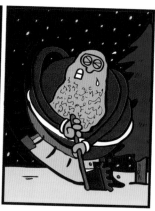

4TH DECEMBER

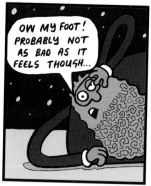

OW MY FOOT! PROBABLY NOT AS BAD AS IT FEELS THOUGH...

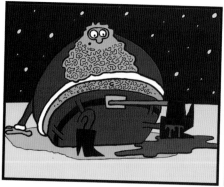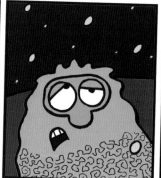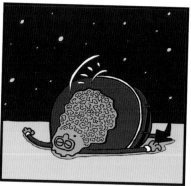

5TH DECEMBER

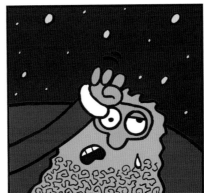

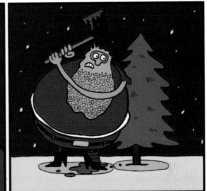

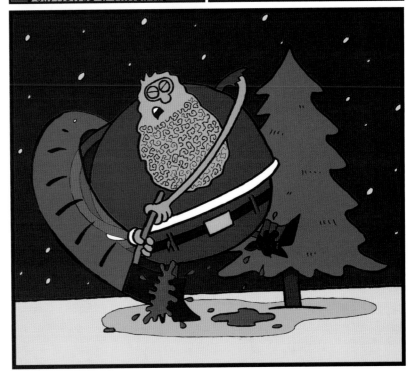

6TH DECEMBER

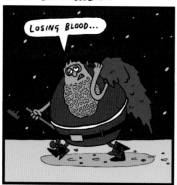
LOSING BLOOD...

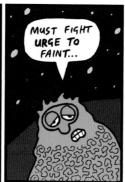
MUST FIGHT URGE TO FAINT...

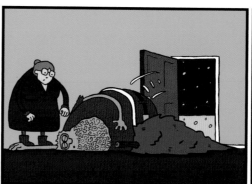

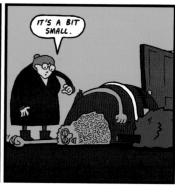
IT'S A BIT SMALL.

7TH DECEMBER

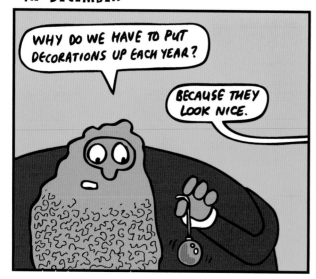
WHY DO WE HAVE TO PUT DECORATIONS UP EACH YEAR?

BECAUSE THEY LOOK NICE.

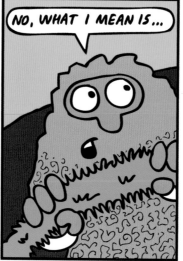
NO, WHAT I MEAN IS...

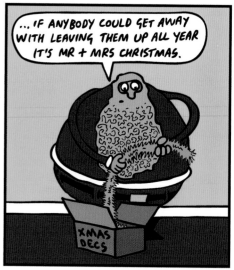
... IF ANYBODY COULD GET AWAY WITH LEAVING THEM UP ALL YEAR IT'S MR + MRS CHRISTMAS.

XMAS DECS

8TH DECEMBER

OW!... MY CENTRAL NERVOUS SYSTEM!

9TH DECEMBER

IT'S FROM THE BLACKMAILER!
AH... THAT'S NICE!
MeRRY XmAS
XXX

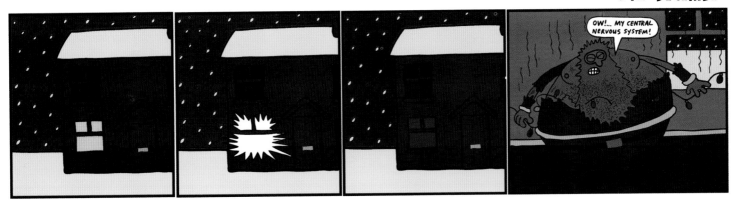

10TH DECEMBER

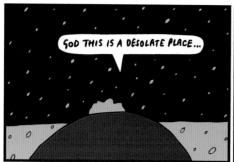 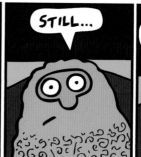 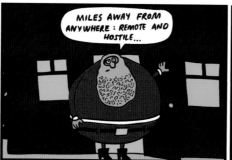 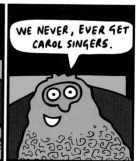

11TH DECEMBER

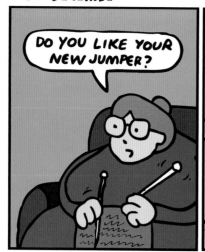 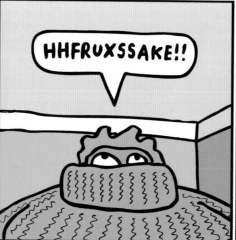 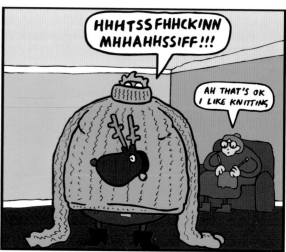

12TH DECEMBER

IS THIS REALLY HOW THE WORLD SEES ME?

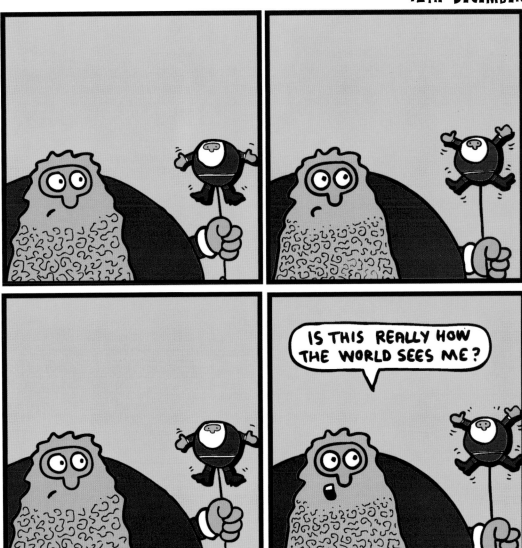

13TH DECEMBER

HO! HO! HO!
HO! HO! HO!
HO! HO!
HOO!!
GOD...
PRETENDING TO BE HAPPY GETS HARDER EVERY YEAR!

14TH DECEMBER

I'LL BE A LAUGHING STOCK IN THIS HAT!
SO IT SHRANK IN THE WASH...
I'LL KNIT YOU A NEW ONE.

15TH DECEMBER

SO WHAT'S THE THEME OF THIS YEAR'S FANCY DRESS PARTY?
SERIOUSLY, BRIAN, ARE YOU RETARDED?

16TH DECEMBER

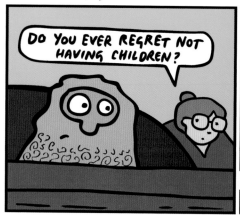

DO YOU EVER REGRET NOT HAVING CHILDREN?

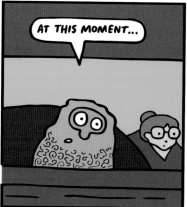

AT THIS MOMENT...

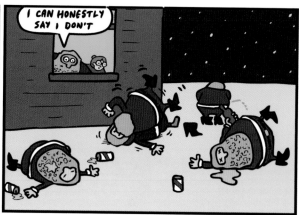

I CAN HONESTLY SAY I DON'T

17TH DECEMBER

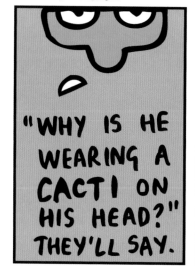

"WHY IS HE WEARING A CACTI ON HIS HEAD?" THEY'LL SAY.

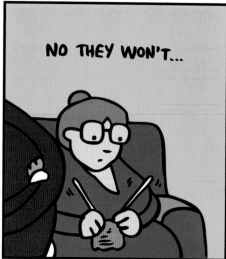

NO THEY WON'T...

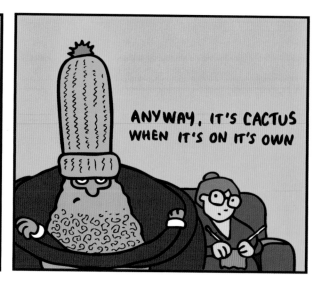

ANYWAY, IT'S CACTUS WHEN IT'S ON IT'S OWN

18TH DECEMBER

I DELIVER GIFTS TO EVERY CHILD ON THE PLANET AND WHAT DO I GET IN RETURN?
HHUH...

19TH DECEMBER

G-NN-ARGH!
I WOULDN'T MIND...
...I DON'T EVEN LIKE PICKLED ONIONS

20TH DECEMBER

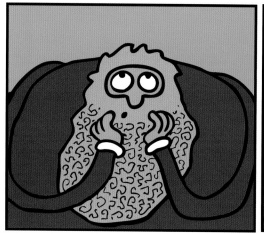

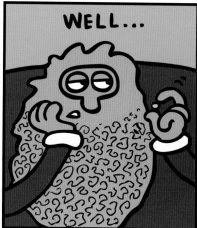

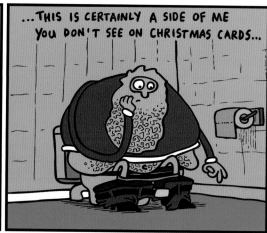

21ST DECEMBER

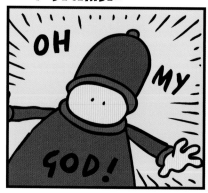

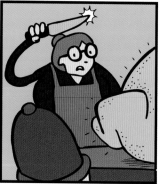

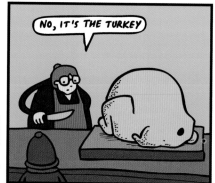

22ND DECEMBER

WHY DO YOU ALWAYS GET SUCH A MASSIVE TURKEY?
IT'S AS BIG AS WE NEED FOR WHO WE'VE INVITED.
WHY, WHO HAVE WE INVITED? LUXEMBOURG?
HA! HA! HA! DID YOU HEAR THAT MARY? LUXEMBOURG!!
MARY?
MARY?

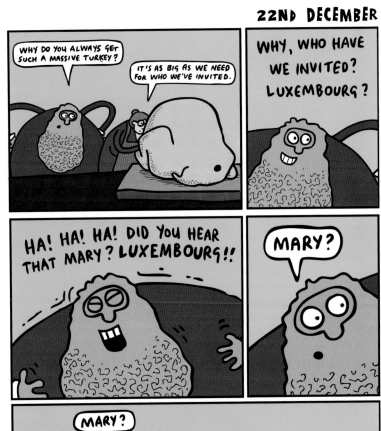

23RD DECEMBER

WORK TOMORROW... HOW DEPRESSING...
BUT THINK OF ALL THE THINGS YOU'VE ACHIEVED WHILE YOU'VE BEEN OFF.
GOD, NOW I'M REALLY DEPRESSED!

24TH DECEMBER

RING! RING!
HELLO?
NO SORRY - HE'S AT WORK...
OH THAT'S A SHAME. HE WOULD HAVE LOVED TO HAVE DONE THAT...
OK THEN... MERRY CHRISTMAS! BYE! BYE!